HOW TO
RETIRE
WITHOUT
RETREATING

Getting Your Ducks in a Row
for a Meaningful Retirement

D0594692

JOHNNIE C. GODWIN

BARBOUR
PUBLISHING

CONTENTS

PREFACE

I accepted the invitation to write this book because I felt like it could make a positive difference in your retirement life or in the lives of those you share retirement with. Now that I've written it, I can honestly say that it has already made a positive difference in my own retirement. How so? After years of retirement, I naturally looked back on the gladnesses and sadnesses of my retirement years, the folly and the fun, the productivity and the futility, and I began to write from experience and perspective. I also began to research books, articles, Internet sites, and the retirement experiences of others to get broader insights and more objectivity to productive retirement. The total process has already enhanced retirement for my wife, Phyllis, and me.

Early on, I decided to take a lifestyle slant in writing the book and not take the road most often traveled of starting with finances and how to make your money last in retirement as long as you do. My publisher and editor were in agreement with my approach. I told them that I wasn't interested in writing a book on 101 things to do in retirement. I was more interested in exploring a balanced retirement of both leisure and productivity as a continuing response to answering one's Christian calling (see Ephesians 4:1).

Speaking about balance, I need to offer a word of explanation and also a caveat to identify the nature of this book. I'm a retired husband who came home to join my homemaking wife, Phyllis. How could such an author be unbiased and provide balance in dealing with retirement for women from all walks of life? There are homemakers, married and single women with careers, those who have never married but are retired survivors in their home, to mention just a few situations. Further, how could one retired male author adequately speak to working couples who retire? There are two-income couples retiring at the same time, at different times, and then a variety of other scenarios for retirement. My answer is that I couldn't be totally unbiased, balanced, experienced, and knowledgeable in all those areas. But I could speak from experience about my own retirement and my homemaking wife's, interview and report other mixes of experience, and try to bring research data into everyday people-talk with conclusions. To the best of my abilities, I've done that.

The book doesn't mean to be gender-biased, though it had to be written by a male or a female—or perhaps coauthored by one of each. In a sense, Phyllis has been my coauthor, offering a woman's perspective. Still, I would ask you to be charitable where I've failed to meet your gender-specific needs or other needs in this book on productive retirement.

Now, after more than a dozen years of retirement and a year spent writing this book, I've decided to take another sabbatical—in the sense that you will read about in the first chapter. Rest from retirement? Rest from productive retirement? Not really. Rather, I've decided to do something different for productive retirement (*Deo volente*). I'm doing some interim pastoring, spending more time on Godwin's Mountain (a special family getaway) with Phyllis, taking some day trips within our own state of Tennessee, planning to visit friends, and hoping to visit family and do more grandparenting. The sabbatical is doing something different and blending leisure, work, and varied new experiences to continue Christian calling but in fresh expressions.

As my friend Elton Trueblood told me more than once, "Each chapter of life is good, and it is good to know in which chapter you are living. I'm living in life's last chapter, and it is best of all." I can say amen to that for my own life as I look back on each chapter and now continue the minichapters in the best chapter of all: *retirement*.

May you join the Author and Finisher of our faith to make your own retirement life's best chapter. And, whatever you do, be sure to choose life (Deuteronomy 30:19).

GENUINELY,
JOHNNIE GODWIN

ACKNOWLEDGMENTS

I own a book whose author chose not to acknowledge anyone for helping him with his book. Perhaps he felt it was best to acknowledge no one rather than risk leaving out someone. Then he dedicated his book with these words: "To No One." I've read lengthy acknowledgments and dedications that would have read better if they had been briefer. I hope to avoid both the extremes of nothingness and too much by acknowledging a few folks who helped most with this volume and by dedicating it to the recipient who seems most worthy of the honor.

First, I dedicate this book to Phyllis, my better two-thirds, who has blessed me in all the chapters of our 48-plus years of marriage and now enriches life's best chapter for both of us. She can read me like a book but doesn't dwell on the bad pages. She can see right through me but loves and cherishes me anyway. And to this very day when people ask me how I got Phyllis, I honestly tell them that I prayed her up. And God gave me the wife I prayed for.

People who've been especially helpful in sharing their own retirement experiences and thoughts truly are numerous. Many of them didn't even know they contributed; and though their names are not here and they're protected by anonymity, they may recognize themselves—or someone else like them. With apologies to all these unmentioned worthies, I nevertheless want to express special gratitude to the help of a few specific people.

I owe my own mentor, James W. Clark, deep appreciation for general tips about retirement and specific suggestions in the area of financial guidelines for retirement. Linda Sandlin has been a constant sounding board and source of input as she and husband Henry often shared both challenges and efforts to deal with them in their own retirement journey. I depended on Oakley and Charline Williams to read chapters about mates entering retirement and then give me their helpful feedback. Phyllis has been my other self and given good wifely counterpoint to her husband's viewpoints on couples and their retirement.

Of course, if it hadn't been for Dad and Mother, I never would have been here to retire anyway. But besides my birth and upbringing, they also gave me retirement insights with Dad's thirteen years of retirement before his death. Then Mother continued to demonstrate for another twelve years what "full" retirement was in her widowhood. And she modeled Christian faith in dying as well as she had in her living. So I'm grateful to my parents for life, retirement life, a faith to live and die by, and a whole lot of what is in this book.

Only a former editor and publisher like me could fully appreciate all that goes into the proposal, contracting, specifying, writing, designing, editing, verifying, proofing, wedding of text and graphics, publishing, publicizing, marketing, and distribution of a book. Thanks to the entire Barbour Publishing, Inc. team for its super help in bringing this book to publication and making it accessible to the reader. Further, a special thanks to Vicki Newby, whose counsel and final editing were a tremendous help to me and, consequently, to the book.

It's traditional for authors to take all responsibility for errors and anything else readers consider blameworthy in a book, and I want to follow that tradition. However, I also ask you to hold anyone noted or quoted blameless for how I've stated their views, misstated their views, muddied what they communicated clearly to me, or skewed the context. Thanks.

Genuinely,

JOHNNIE C. GODWIN

CHAPTER ONE

TAKE A SABBATICAL

Days of respite are golden days.

ROBERT SOUTH

Whatever else retirement may be, it is to be a respite—a plateau of rest from the press and stress of climbing life's daily mountains. A retirement respite is a change from living life exactly as you have lived it in its earlier chapters. Retirement is a new journey in the pilgrimage of life. Though countless others have made this journey and will gladly counsel you how to make the trip, your own retirement will be a unique trip you'll have to experience for yourself.

However, you'll likely find some good pointers as you read here what I and others have mapped out and noted on our own retirement journeys up to this point. Of course, how you make the trip and arrive at the final destination is up to you. But when you do come to the end of retirement, I hope you'll be able to say that the last chapter—no matter how difficult—was best of all and that the respite was golden.

THE CHAPTER OF LIFE TITLED *RETIREMENT*

Regardless of what has brought you to the chapter of life titled *Retirement*, it's a good idea to take a sabbatical. The root meaning of *sabbatical* is to cease, desist, or rest. After lengthy, productive, and tiring work, people profit by a rest. And after a lifetime of labor, retirement offers the chance for changes of pace, activity, pursuits, and maybe even location.

What brings a person to the momentous occasion of retirement probably affects the person's feelings and attitudes about retirement. After having a career in one field or a long-time job in one type of work, retirement introduces sudden change. So whether retirement comes by choice, downsizing, health problems, or whatever, the new experience of not having a regular job may cause you to feel euphoria, grief, confusion, anxiety, or something else. Regardless of why you retired and what your feelings are, the time is yours. You can choose to do what you want to do.

It's okay to rest. God, who paused after His creation, gave the Sabbath for humankind to do likewise. And when Jesus was tired, even He paused to rest (John 4:6).

With retirement freedom often comes an emotional high. Enjoy that euphoric experience of the lightness of being. On the other hand, for various reasons, some retirees experience a sense of grief, puzzlement, or lostness. A sabbatical provides time to deal with grief that may come with separation from a long-term job, long-term friends, and having a place where you feel you belong.

Newfound freedom from the shackles of schedules and agendas may leave you with a blank page to write life's next chapter on, and you don't know what to write. You may just be exhausted and need rest. For some period of time, it seems wise to take a sabbatical. I'm not recommending indulgent retirement but a sabbatical starting point that may have some indulgence involved in it.

PRESIDENTIAL PRECEDENTS

When President Jimmy Carter was just fifty-six years old, he was involuntarily retired from his position. He and wife Rosalynn were embarrassed, broke, despairing, and felt that their productive lives were about over—although they might live another thirty years or more. Later, President Carter wrote: "For a while we just paused and contemplated our lives. To pass the time, we laid down a floor in our attic, became reacquainted with our farmland, and jogged or took long bike rides through the countryside, stopping to visit at the homes of our friends of past years" (*The Virtues of Aging*).

So the Carters began retirement with a sabbatical. They didn't become sedentary couch potatoes; rather, they departed from all-consuming work and rested by doing something different. For them that was a productive time. And since then, whatever political judgments anyone has made, popular opinion seems to be that Jimmy Carter is one of our best ex-presidents as he lives retirement life meaningfully and productively with greater variety than he ever knew before in all his life.

George H. W. Bush was the first member of that family to become president. And after one term, he was defeated. He and wife Barbara and family members faced feelings that were different but in some ways like the Carters. In the gloom-and-doom atmosphere that continued to hang over the family after the defeat, it was reported that Barbara Bush said something like this: "It's over; get over it." And the family did get over it during that sabbatical and rediscovered life and joy and productivity. And, of course, they were vicariously reelected when their son George W. was elected as the second President Bush.

In all of life, sabbaticals are needed; but they're especially needed in defeat and grief. Though these two presidential sabbaticals were forced sabbaticals, they are examples of life beyond retirement from the White House. Further, these two high-profile sabbaticals are instructive to us regular folks who have an equally great need to discover that retirement can be great. There is more to add to the resume for those who want to add to it—after a sabbatical.

PERSONAL PRIVILEGE—A BIT OF SHARING

Both work and retirement started early for me. As a seven-year-old boy, I began selling newspapers on the streets of my west Texas hometown of Midland. And I worked hard all of my life until 1992. Then overnight I was suddenly downsized at age fifty-five—much earlier than I had ever dreamed of retiring. But I wasn't alone. Between 1990 and 1997, twenty-one million others also lost their jobs to downsizing (*Reader's Digest*, Feb. 1999). And since then millions more have lost their jobs through downsizing, job deletions, corporate bankruptcy scandals, the effects of terrorism, and economic ups and downs.

In my moment of being downsized, I was summoned to a no-preparation-required meeting toward the end of a workday. At the meeting, the corporate officer I answered to and the human resources director broke the news of my downsizing to me. No one had said anything about downsizing in our corporation, and I myself was a vice president in good standing: no bad marks; good performance, results, and relationships.

So I was stunned as the officer commended me on my fine career and excellent work but told of the board of trustees' mandate for new leadership in our corporation. My twenty-two-plus years of hard work in six upwardly mobile positions in the corporation and my loyalty to it received a thanks and an explanation of my retirement benefits, which were certainly fair. I personally had nothing to do with the downsizing. A change in corporate culture was the culprit, and I was just the first of many to get shocked with the downsizing news.

As I had listened in silence, the numbness of shock turned to feelings of anger, grief, disappointment, chagrin, acceptance, and finally relief. Then it was quiet and my time to speak. I told these two colleagues of mine that I knew it had been hard for them to break the news to me. Further, I told them I knew it would be hard for them to give that same message to others who were my peers.

Then I took over the meeting by concluding it with prayer for those two guys. After my amen, I looked them in the eye, shook their hands, and left—and we're still friends. I'll tell you more about how this event that seemed to be a tragedy later proved to be a blessing in disguise. But for now, I'll just share that I went back to my office, sat alone, and began to get myself together for a while.

Then I went home. A lifetime rule at my house has been that we don't ever share bad news until after dinner. Our three sons were grown and gone. So wife Phyllis and I ate dinner and exchanged a bit of general conversation about the day, just as we always did. After dinner, I told her I had news that would sound bad at the beginning but would be good at the end. I told her I needed to talk with her about my retirement.

With shock on her face and anxiety in her heart, she asked, "When?"

I said, "Now."

Phyllis teared up with shock, concern, and whatever else brings tears. Our feelings were similar to those of the Carters, the Bushes, millions of others, and perhaps yours.

With urgency in her voice, Phyllis wanted to know what we would do. Without her knowing details about the retirement, the question was a natural one. In so many words, I told her that I didn't know over the long haul what we would do but that for the rest of that year we would take a sabbatical. And we did.

Whether your retirement is voluntary or involuntary, full retirement or semiretirement, I would still recommend a sabbatical. Some people equate a sabbatical with having lots of money or a good position or both. We did have some severance pay, but I no longer had a position. So perhaps some more explanation about our first-year sabbatical and types of sabbaticals might be helpful.

A SUPER SABBATICAL

Before inflation could affect us or other things could bog us down, Phyllis and I took off for part of a year to do things we had only dreamed about before. We got a good travel deal and with severance pay went on our first cruise. We hadn't been pampered like that since we were babies. The food was so rich and varied that Phyllis was embarrassed midweek when I asked in one of the swanky dining rooms if I could just have a plain old cheeseburger. They answered I could, and I did. For Phyllis and me, it was another honeymoon after more than thirty-five years of marriage, and we began to get to know each other again without the phone ringing or a schedule to meet or a place to go.

That was the beginning of our sabbatical, though your sabbatical might be completely different from ours. We had saved some money and were travel-wise in getting bargain fares. But the point of a sabbatical is not how long it lasts, how far or frequently you travel, or how much money you spend. (See chapter 14, "Outliving Your Money?" for more insights on this matter.) The point of a sabbatical is a rest and a change from what you've been doing.

When we got back home and settled in, I joined Phyllis for her daily three-mile walk in our subdivision as a continuation of the sabbatical. As we walked, I discovered that a vacant one-acre lot we passed several times each day was for sale. The lot was a swampy eyesore to the subdivision. The ground wouldn't percolate and couldn't pass county health requirements for building a house on it. But the faded FOR SALE sign had a phone number I memorized. I investigated the asking price, made a ridiculously low offer, and was surprised to have it accepted. So I bought the lot—much to Phyllis's chagrin.

Then I began to improve the lot by cutting down junk trees, mowing grass, and "nicing it up" in general. I formed a team of everyone who had to be involved in improving and approving the lot for house building and in meeting our subdivision's covenants. A thing called a *curtain drain* had to be installed to handle the lack of percolation. So I got that and everything else called for. In time, the needed approvals came through, and I sold the lot for a tidy profit. Today there's a neat house with fine landscaping where that old swamp was. Now, that manual labor may not sound like a sabbatical to you, but it was a sabbatical to me because it was different and a type of rest from corporate work. Besides all that, the activity kept me off the street and out of Phyllis's kitchen.

With frequent-flyer miles I had been saving, we took a trip to Aruba, where the trees are bent almost flat from the constant winds. We snorkeled and hiked and shopped. We drove around and looked at the wild goats and the wild tourists. Before memories of that trip had time to get dim, we discovered a $448 roundtrip flight to Madrid, Spain, from Nashville, Tennessee. Now, I had always wanted to go to Spain. So we went. Besides doing the tourist bit for twelve days in a rental car, we took missionaries out to eat wherever we visited and encouraged them.

Besides that, I was able to confirm an old preacher story I had doubted, about an ancient aqueduct in Segovia still operating today. The only threat to the aqueduct's existence had been a short time of retiring it for posterity rather than using it. But since disuse was destroying what time and usage had not hurt, the aqueduct was put back into use. The story was true and contains a seed of truth for retirement itself.

In between trips, I became proficient on an Internet travel bulletin board and learned more about the U.S. Virgin Island of St. John than most of its natives know. Then we flew to St. Thomas and took the ferry over for an isolated week on St. John. We got a 20 percent discount off our hotel with the senior citizen AARP card. Again we snorkeled in beautiful waters, shopped for souvenirs, and ate dinner with friends we had met only over the Internet bulletin board. We learned what it was like to be without a phone, a notebook computer, or a pager. We were incommunicado for the first time in all the years we could remember. No one knew us, and no one could reach us.

We enjoyed the sabbatical experiences of our first retirement year, and they helped prepare us for a productive retirement. However, it's worth inserting that sabbaticals are supposed to be recurring experiences. Further, sabbaticals don't have to be long in duration, extensive in travel, or expensive in cost. They can be taken in your own backyard, so to speak. We've continued to find joy in taking minisabbaticals.

MINISABBATICALS

Though it might have sounded as if we were rich in that first year of retirement travel, we weren't. Rather, we were fortunate to have had some extra income for a brief time. But it wasn't the money that made the sabbatical; it was the doing something different and the rest involved. Since then, we have saved money from time to time for a week or two of sabbaticals. We joined a travel club and got special deals and access to good bargains that come with getting old enough to retire. And we've traveled closer to home and enjoyed car trips to visit friends and relatives and to take roads less traveled out in the boonies of Tennessee and Kentucky.

Regardless of money available, almost everyone can take a sabbatical of some kind—of some length. You don't really even have to leave home to take a sabbatical. You can stay at home or close by and not travel far to experience a minisabbatical. In fact, some people who retire are so tired of traveling that planes and other kinds of travel remind them of work. So, to them, spending time in the garden or flower bed might be a type of sabbatical—a rest of something different from career work. Hiking, playing tennis, and moseying around, and a lot of other fun activities don't cost much.

We found that minisabbaticals are lots of fun. You can take day trips to explore sights nearby and be back in your own bed and on your own pillow by nighttime. Or you can put just a couple of days together and explore your own region or state. We did that when we drove across the Cherohala Skyway from southeast Tennessee to North Carolina. We had only read about the Skyway in a magazine. On that trip, we spent a night in a quaint North Carolina town and drove on to Blowing Rock, North Carolina. That's where Jan Karon, author of The Mitford Series, lived as she wrote, and we wanted to see the cultural backdrop for her books.

Closer to home, we have found sabbatical relaxation by working at something totally different from career work. Our three sons and their families each gave us one hundred dollars at retirement to go toward a toolshed to put on Godwin's Mountain. (Godwin's Mountain is fifty-six nearby acres we bought about twenty-five years ago but hadn't gotten to fully enjoy because of career work and lack of time.) We felt a little guilty taking the hard-earned money from our boys and their families, but it was a gift not to be refused. Gradually, as I looked at display models of wooden sheds to be built on-site, I started with the smallest model and continued to look until I came to the two-story model. It's a Godwin guy thing that bigger is better, so that's the one we bought—but not for the three hundred dollars. The shell-of-a-cabin was sixteen feet by twenty-four feet, and we got it built on the very top of our mountain.

That was the beginning of both rest and work away from

civilization—no running water, no bathroom facilities, and no light except by lantern or generator. We worked like dogs to make that place a good getaway, but it was pure fun. The work was part of our sabbatical rest. The main thing is resting from career work and doing something different, something that departs from the normal routine.

As Daniel Considine said, "Find out for yourself the form of rest that refreshes you best." And I would add, enjoy the blessed rest without guilt.

SABBATICALS WITHOUT GUILT

"It is no disgrace to rest a bit."

GENE FOWLER

Many enter retirement without an awareness that they have become workaholics. In fact, it may take retirement for you to discover that you've let yourself become a workaholic. Psychologist Wayne Oates gave us the word *workaholic*, but throughout history many others have described the addiction. Stephen MacKenna said, "I find I haven't the art of rest." Ernest Hello wrote, "To work is simple enough; but to rest, there is the difficulty." George Ade said, "One cannot rest except after steady practice" (*Forty Modern Fables*). Benjamin Franklin said, "He that can take rest is greater than he that can take cities."

And as far as taking a sabbatical without guilt goes, I agree with St. John Baptiste de La Salle: "God. . .authorizes us to take that rest and refreshment which are necessary to keeping up the strength of mind and body." Grenville Kleiser said, "Periods of wholesome laziness, after days of energetic effort, will wonderfully tone up the mind and body." Almost everyone knows the truth of what Ovid wrote: "A field that has rested gives a bountiful crop." And as Dagwood Bumstead said in a cartoon after one of his naps, "The power is back on." And in my retirement mode, I didn't need an explanation.

SABBATICALS HAVE REASONS

Leo Tolstoy wrote, "In the name of God, stop a moment, cease your work, look around you." Mortimer Adler said, "When I have nothing to do for an hour, and I don't want to do anything, I neither read nor watch television. I sit back in a chair and let my mind relax. I do what I call idling. It's as if the motorcar's running but you haven't got it in gear. You have to allow a certain amount of time in which you are doing nothing in order to have things occur to you, to let your mind think."

Henry Ford once hired an efficiency expert to analyze his company. After some time of observation, the expert gave a positive report on almost everything he saw. However, he mentioned that he had noticed that one man a few offices away from Ford's was always kicked back with his feet on the desk and doing nothing. Ford commented, "That man once had an idea that saved our company millions of dollars, and if I remember correctly, his feet were in the same position then."

Idleness may be only apparent and not real. The wheels of the mind can whir in silence and stillness under the guise of laziness. From my own experience, I can amen that it is important to learn to say yes to times of productive inactivity.

On Godwin's Mountain, we have a large cave we love to explore. There's no need to fear running into any animals after the first couple of rooms, because they don't venture into total darkness and stay there. We see a few bats that have their own radar and come outside toward nightfall. Other critters are albino salamanders. They have no color and seemingly no vision. You see, living in total darkness means living a life without color, vision, or light.

Many folks live in a colorless cave of darkness without vision, insight, or perspective. They need a sabbatical. It can be a year, six months, a month, or even a week or two. A sabbatical helps us back off, evaluate priorities, get perspective, and decide how to live life—especially retirement life. For us to know how we want to live retirement life in the twenty-first century, we need to know the alternatives and be bold enough to choose what to leave the same and what to change. A sabbatical can help pave the way for good retirement planning and decisions.

A sabbatical itself is medicine to the soul. Thomas Carlyle wrote, "Rest is a fine medicine." And Harold J. Reilly ventured to claim, "Rest has cured more people than all the medicine in the world." For these reasons and more, I say, take a sabbatical when you retire.

SABBATICALS ARE FOR A SEASON

Sabbaticals are not retirement. They are only for a season. *Sabbaticals are always from something, for something, and to something.* In the academic world and later in the business world, sabbaticals were introduced as recurring leaves of absence. The purposes of sabbaticals were rest, renewal, travel, study, writing, training, service, and acquiring of new skills. They were not intended to be unending vacations of idleness.

Homer said, "Too much rest itself becomes a pain." Blaise Pascal wrote, "Our nature consists in motion; complete rest is death." And Ovid wrote, "Alternate rest and labor long endure."

CONCLUSION

Ideally, the beginning of retirement will include a sabbatical of rest, relaxation, and doing something different from what you retired from. The kind of sabbatical you choose needs to fit you and your resources. The value of a sabbatical doesn't depend on its length or luxury but on a rest from the work you've been doing and a recharging to enable you to come back to a new kind of productivity. In that way, the sabbatical itself is productive.

REFLECTIONS AND PROJECTIONS

- Reflect on all the jobs and kinds of work you ever did. Which were the best? Which were the worst? These reflections might help in your retirement projections.
- Recall your best vacations, holidays, and sabbaticals.
- What have you envisioned your retirement to consist of?
- Identify retirement plans you've already made and evaluate whether they're adequate for living life's next chapters that could last twenty-five years or more.
- Seriously consider a planned sabbatical (1) to rest from career work, (2) to get the feel of almost 100 percent optional time, and (3) to consider all the retirement possibilities that naturally begin to pop into a retiree's mind while the motor idles.
- Keep a retirement diary or journal (1) to record retirement happenings you may not otherwise remember; (2) to retain thoughts, ideas, and plans that may come to you; and (3) to provide a log of what could be a happy and productive retirement and a retirement map for your children and grandchildren to read and evaluate.

RETIREMENT WORDS FROM THE WORD
Mark 2:27; Matthew 25:23; Matthew 11:28

PRAYER THOUGHTS
Father, grant us a sabbatical "far from the madding crowd's ignoble strife" (Thomas Gray). Help us to "rest. . .till the Master of all good workmen shall put us to work anew" (Rudyard Kipling). We thank You for creating labor and crowning it with rest. Amen.

CHAPTER TWO

AFTER THE EUPHORIA IS OVER

Absence of occupation is not rest;
a mind quite vacant is a mind distressed.

WILLIAM COWPER

Euphoria means a feeling of great happiness or well-being. It's how we feel in life's super moments and during mountaintop experiences. Marriages and honeymoons are times of euphoria. Graduations bring degrees of euphoria. Anticipating a vacation builds into euphoria.

But as wonderful and exhilarating as these and other feel-good experiences are, euphoria is only temporary. After the euphoria is over, we usually return to some kind of regular daily living that includes ruts and routines. We spend most of our life somewhere between the valleys and the mountaintops. And realistically that's true of retirement, too. But there's a lot of difference between retiring from a job and retiring from life. This book isn't about retiring from life but moving to a higher level of joy and productivity. So let's take a look at the rites of retirement and consider what to do after the euphoria is over.

RITES OF RETIREMENT

The announcement of retirement usually results in a fairly predictable pattern of events—with some exceptions for downsizings, forced retirements, and so forth. As people enter the final year of work, they begin to sense the things they will do for the last time. Then the fact of retirement begins to occur.

The typical scenario might be something like this: a reception for the retiree, letters from colleagues and friends, recognition for accomplishments, a plaque to hang on the wall, maybe a bonus, a final paycheck, an exit interview that explains postemployment benefits, turning in keys and credit cards, and then taking your own stuff home. There are some poignant moments and lots of nostalgic ones. But then it's party time—or euphoria time.

Planned retirement almost inevitably has a time of euphoria about it. Although unplanned retirement may have grief in it and compress the rites of retirement, there's still some exhilaration about retiring. There is a break with the past, and the retiree enters uncharted waters. Even though the new adventure might be scary and carry anxieties with it, there is still an excitement that stirs the blood and causes the heart to beat a little faster. The feeling might be compared to getting out of school for summer vacation; but in this case, it is getting out of school for the rest of your life. What euphoria! What exhilaration!

When my dad retired, he didn't do anything for six months. Well, that's not exactly true. He stayed in bed and read and watched endless hours of TV. (The average older person now watches over forty hours of TV each week.) Dad did interrupt his rest to eat meals, drink coffee with friends at McDonald's, go to garage sales, and attend church. Most of our family members were greatly concerned that Dad would wither away and die because of his inactivity. I wasn't really worried, because I knew he was just taking a sabbatical.

When Dad retired, he commented that he had worked hard all of his life and had done what others wanted him to do; now he was going to do what he wanted to do. And he did. But after about six months, it was almost like the moment when Forrest Gump decided to quit running. Dad quit doing nothing and started doing things again.

He had been a truck driver, and he started driving the church bus on trips. He struck up a friendship with owners of a mattress company and found himself enjoying short-haul deliveries for them. Even when he could no longer do those things because age-related blindness overtook him, he learned something every day by listening to recorded books far into the night. His curiosity was still alive the last week of his life, and he was still asking questions to learn new things. Dad kept his sense of humor that blessed the lives of others. And he had a meaningful retirement until the day he died in good health at age seventy-eight.

If the retiree follows the typical pattern, there's at least some time for pure sabbatical pleasure upon retirement. Then, after living it up, comes the settling down and finding out what retirement is all about. When the passage from work to retirement has been made and the honeymoon of sabbatical is over, the euphoria will be over also. What then? That is the retirement question.

PARADIGMS THAT DON'T PAN OUT

A paradigm is a pattern, a model, a template to go by. Each person's retirement may be as unique as his fingerprints in some ways. However, there are common approaches to retirement that we might call "retirement paradigms." And at the front end of retirement, it's worthwhile to know which paradigms to avoid and which factors to include in your own retirement paradigm.

A holiday every day? One friend of mine retired with plans to play golf every day for the rest of his life. And he did play golf almost every day for six months. Then golf got to be more like going to work than going on vacation. He wasn't happy with his retirement dream. So after thinking things over and looking around for a while, he decided to go back to work. Oh, not the suit-and-necktie corporate life he had known. He became the engineer on a train in an amusement park and loved it. There he was in his bib overalls, red handkerchief around his neck, wearing an engineer's cap, and making kids and their parents happy. It made him happy, too.

My friend Copper Daugherty put it another way after his first year of retirement. He said, "Johnnie, this retirement business is not all it's cracked up to be. I used to look forward to weekends, holidays, and vacations. Now there's nothing to take a vacation from." God made us for alternate work and rest, and without some kind of productive work, rest leaves us restless. As George Bernard Shaw once wrote, "A perpetual holiday is a good working definition of hell" (*Misalliance*).

Aimless diversions. Besides the misconception of retirement as a perennial holiday, another paradigm that doesn't pan out is the unplanned retirement of aimless diversions. Lots of people who retire don't plan to indulge themselves in the hedonism of pleasure and no work. They just know they don't want to punch a clock or take orders anymore. They want to be free to do what they want to do even though they don't know what it is. As they search for meaning in retirement, some of them gravitate toward shopping malls, garage sales, or coffee-drinking gatherings.

Others let time disappear by trying to decide what to do. You can usually spot aimless-diversion retirees because they tend to look bored, empty, guilty, and lost or uncertain of where they're going.

Balloon mortgage approach. I didn't know what a balloon mortgage was until I bought some property and soon decided against that choice. In a nutshell, the balloon mortgage process allows a buyer to pay a relatively small sum during the front end and ensuing years of a mortgage while enjoying the use of the purchase now. But when the term of the mortgage is up, everything owed is due at once in one "balloon payment," which usually is a large sum.

Many people look at life and retirement in a similar way. They sell their soul to a company store or a life of drudgery or just plain old work to make a living. Their vacations may be sparse and their savings large because of the expected balloon payoff of a super retirement. They sacrifice for their dream of a balloon-payoff retirement and feel entitled to it. In other words, they put up with anything and everything along life's way in exchange for their dream of a pot of gold at retirement. And they expect it to be a long retirement.

At least two things are wrong with this paradigm. First, the person who does not learn a lifestyle of ongoing joy and variety before retirement likely will not learn to enjoy life fully in retirement. The second thing wrong with this paradigm is that it fails to deal with human mortality and God's will (see James 4:13–17). Death, poor health, economic disaster, or some other circumstance may interrupt the big payoff. The best preparation for retirement and old age is to live a faith-filled life and celebrate each day along the way. Even an early death can't take away the fullness of the life you've already lived.

The boredom/old-age paradigm. I've noticed that those who are bored seem readier to die sooner than those who are alive with life. Some of these folks pay more attention to the calendar and their number of years than they do to joyful and productive living. They increasingly begin to talk or think about how old they are. One person told me, "People don't realize how old I'm getting to be." Another individual sadly commented, "This may be my last Christmas." With a tone of boredom, one retiree said, "I guess I'm ready for Freddy." None of these people got much older; they soon died. Marie Ray said, "No one grows old by living—only by losing interest in living."

Voltaire said, "Rest is a good thing, but boredom is its brother." Those who retire to do nothing and do it may get bored to death. Then when they get bored and stay bored, nature seems to accommodate their readiness to die. But those who keep on finding purpose and excitement in life also tend to keep on living longer. Further, they stay lively and keep on enjoying a better quality of life. They grow older, but they never seem to be old. They're interested in others and aren't preoccupied with themselves, their health, and when they're going to die. As they live outside themselves and live for others, they seem to extend and enrich their own lives, too.

The Right Retirement Paradigm

There's nothing wrong with anticipating retirement and entering it with excitement, joy, and expectancy. Chances are, most retirees have accented work far more than rest up to the retirement point in their lives. So it's okay for retirement to be a time of syncopating life by shortening the work and accenting the leisure. It's all right to devote more time to family, travel, sports, hobbies, recreation, and personal plans to be happy.

God gives us blessings to enjoy: "The living God. . .giveth us richly all things to enjoy" (1 Timothy 6:17 KJV). Retirement is one of those blessed things He gives us. Of course, God also blesses us so we can bless others, and retirement is one of those blessings to share.

The main point here is that retirement paradigms don't pan out when they consist primarily of self-indulgence or unproductive aimlessness. Such lifestyles are seldom, if ever, satisfying for long. Helen Keller said, "Life is either a daring adventure or nothing. To keep our faces toward change and behave like free spirits in the presence of fate is strength undefeatable." A successful retirement paradigm involves daring adventure, freedom to choose, and a willingness to face change and, yes, even initiate it.

Retirement does not come in one size that fits all. However, there is a right paradigm that models principles to include in every retirement. I'll get more into that in the next chapter on *Deo volente*, but for now, it is enough to say that the right paradigm doesn't include the selfishness of self-centered indulgence. The right paradigm does include a shifting accent to rest, a changing melody that still includes work, the music of hope, and faith to dance to it. The right paradigm calls for learning what to do meaningfully with time.

LEARNING TO KILL TIME?

Retiree friend Jim Clark told me that his father had instilled within him at an early age the need to prepare for retirement financially. So Jim did. But no one ever told him the great need to prepare for how to use all the time he would have in retirement.

A retiree has many transitions to make, but chances are he'll make most of them okay and have help doing it. Whether it's dealing with financial matters, insurance, health concerns, housing, transportation, or whatever, most retirees manage to work through the processes one way or the other. But what to do with time in retirement is another matter.

Physician Paul Tournier wrote, "What each of us needs is a reconversion from earning our living to cultural activity" (*Learn to Grow Old*). By this, Tournier was referring to the need to move from working for a living to building a retirement life filled with significance and meaning. He pointed out that many people seem to feel leisure calls for finding a way to kill time without getting too bored. Instead, he wrote that retirement's leisure ideally should be used for self-development, progress, contribution to the human race, and finding meaning in life that survives professional activity.

Tournier envisioned retirement as a time of growth and productivity. Not a time of having to hunt for something to fill time. Not a time when family and friends try to ease you into the mold they think you should occupy in retirement. Tournier said that the problem for retirees is not filling up time; rather, it is filling time with that which is significant and meaningful for them.

Long ago, I read this proverb: "You can't kill time without injuring eternity." For me, the divine stewardship of life is at the heart of what to do with retirement time.

A DEVELOPMENTAL TASK

As in the first part of life, all of retirement is a developmental task—one of life's hurdles—that calls for making wise choices.

While still at the front end of retirement, it's wise to make a conscious decision to live on the topside of life rather than underneath it. It is realistic to face the fact that in retirement we will inevitably decline physically and suffer losses. Sara Teasdale wrote, "I make the most of all that comes and the least of all that goes." In essence, she was saying that she had learned to make gratitude greater than grief in her life. She chose to welcome and give thanks for her blessings rather than wallow in despair and regret. Making retirement life's best chapter is largely a matter of attitude.

We have the developmental task of choosing what our attitudes and approaches will be in retirement. We can decide ahead of time to give thanks for the light rather than curse the darkness—to pass through the dark night of the soul to experience new sunrises. We can choose to experience enrichment and add to our lives if we will say yes to change and opportunity.

We have the choice to learn how to make the most of time and the least of our losses. So after the retirement euphoria is over, it's time to begin writing life's next chapter (with the help of the Author and Finisher of our faith).

REFLECTIONS AND PROJECTIONS

- Take a personality inventory. At retirement, you may have as much as one-third of your life left to live. So it's a good idea to know your options regarding how to live that long chapter of life and each of its minichapters.

- What did you once enjoy doing that you quit doing and would like to restart?

- What new thing do you want to start doing?

- What are you interested in doing but not equipped to do right now?

- How do you plan to mesh your retirement life with your mate's—who may or may not be retired—life?

RETIREMENT WORDS FROM THE WORD

Matthew 25:25–26, 28; Proverbs 3:5; Proverbs 6:9; Philippians 4:8–9; 1 Thessalonians 5:18.

PRAYER THOUGHTS

Father, help me to remember the past with joy but not to live in it. Remind me that You are not through remolding me into Your image. Help me to balance rest, recreation, and work. May I be aware that Your will includes earthly rest but not retirement from Your will and Your unending call. With hope and faith, I commit my retirement life to You. Amen.

CHAPTER THREE

WRITING LIFE'S NEXT CHAPTER

Just don't leave it unwritten.

CHUCK MORRIS

As I think back to the first year or two of retirement, I can see how God was working to guide me into a different but productive era of life. Even while I was on sabbatical and thinking about what to do with retirement, God was using past friendships and experiences as a bridge to the future. Although retirement was uncharted territory, Phyllis and I weren't starting from square one.

Retirees have a foundation to build on regardless of how different retirement life may be from earlier years. And for Christians, the same One who guided them in earlier years is there to continue with His guidance. The pages of life's retirement chapters are blank, but the research for further writing is largely already done. So it's time to begin again.

AN UNWRITTEN CHAPTER

For the next few weeks after my involuntary retirement, my diary reads that I was praying to know what the Lord would have me write in life's next chapter. During that time, Phyllis went to a missions week at a conference center along with some other women. Longtime friends Chuck and Erica Morris were among the missionaries attending the conference. My downsized retirement was common knowledge, so Chuck asked Phyllis what I planned to do next. Phyllis answered with what she had heard me say: "He's praying to know what to write in life's next chapter."

Chuck nodded but counseled, "Tell him that I said, 'Just don't leave it unwritten.'"

When Phyllis brought the message home, it made an indelible impression on me. I realized the importance of planning, deciding, and getting on with the retirement chapter of life, or else it would be unwritten. I had no control over my downsizing, and I haven't had any control over many other circumstances in life. Life's circumstances can crush us or be kind to us without our choice, but we can choose what we will write on each page of life's last chapter to make it the best chapter.

A TEXT FOR THE NEW CHAPTER

A publisher friend named Art Van Eck called to see how I was doing and to invite me to do some paid consulting for his organization. As we talked about retirement, time, and what to do in the future, I mentioned that in life's pilgrimage, I had a scripture for every major turning point. Art asked, "What is the scripture for now?" I didn't have to pause for thought to give an answer. I had been reading Ephesians and told him it was Ephesians 4:1 (my translation, my emphasis): "I, Paul, a prisoner of the Lord, *call* you alongside me to walk worthy of the *calling* wherein you are *called*." In the Greek text of that verse, Paul used a form of *call* three times in one verse. It's easy to see that Paul was talking about God calling us to do His calling, which really is our unending vocation—regardless of what we do to make a living.

Retirement may mean the end of a job, but it's not the end of a Christian's spiritual vocation. And I knew that though my job had changed, my calling hadn't. So when I was involuntarily retired, I told people I wasn't looking for a job but was trying to fulfill a calling.

YOUR OTHER VOCATION

This fact of God's calling is not just something for preacher types, missionaries, or denominational workers to answer as a career calling and to continue to answer in retirement. This calling is not just for men; it is for all Christians regardless of sex, age, skills, aptitudes, or other factors. Speaking of all Christians, Paul wrote, "God. . .hath given to us the ministry of reconciliation" (2 Corinthians 5:18 KJV). That is the thesis of Elton Trueblood's book titled *Your Other Vocation*.

No matter what any of us does to make a living or serve in the home or elsewhere, our primary vocation is the calling of God for us to work with Him in the ministry of reconciliation. "We'll Work Till Jesus Comes" is not just a song for preachers. No Christian retiree has the option of abandoning God's vocational calling to His service or His church (which Christ loved and gave Himself for).

There is an unchanging fact in the Christian calling that transcends all of life, including retirement. The fact is that every chapter of life is to begin with God rather than with self. And that's especially true of the retirement chapter. So let's get to the beginning and the heart of what productive retirement is all about.

DEO VOLENTE

Latin may have filtered out to west Texas by the time of my growing-up days there, but none of it seeped into my experience. However, as I left home for further schooling, I began to read the phrase *Deo volente*, or the initials D.V., in books that were written in English. After some time, I discovered that the Latin words or initials stood for "God willing." For hundreds of years, people with wisdom have used *Deo volente* to note that their plans and their very lives are subject to God's will. Ever since I learned about *Deo volente*, I, too, have added the term to all of my goals and to the writings of my personal diary. The phrase is not a platitude but a foundation, an awareness, and a starting point.

The Bible underlines the need to consider God's will as the foundation for planning any chapter of life. In fact, there won't even be another chapter of life unless God wills it. The book of James says, "Now listen, you who say, 'Today or tomorrow we will go to this or that city, spend a year there, carry on business and make money.' Why, you do not even know what will happen tomorrow. What is your life? You are a mist that appears for a little while and then vanishes. Instead, you ought to say, 'If it is the Lord's will, we will live and do this or that'" (James 4:13–15 NIV).

It is foolish to plan retirement without first going to God for His will. The scripture's point and my point is to guard against making our plans and then presenting them to God for His stamp of approval. The emphasis is on going to God first and repeatedly to discover what His will is for us and then doing that will. Matthew 6:33 (KJV) says, "Seek ye first the kingdom of God, and his righteousness; and all these things shall be added unto you." Well, as you think about retirement, how does what you've just read square with "What things soever ye desire, when ye pray, believe that ye receive them, and ye shall have them" (Mark 11:24 KJV)?

The right paradigm or pattern for retirement is to start with the blueprints of the One who created us and designed our lives to be lived in His image. And He has some blessings for us we will not receive unless we ask for them. When we go to the Author and Finisher of our faith for guidance, we are also most likely to find what our hearts really desire.

The supreme test for our heart's desire in retirement is to test what we want in light of what God wants for us. It's a mystery, but what God actually unfolds for us is better than our greatest dreams. That's true for all of life, but it has become more apparent to me in retirement.

THE UNFOLDING DRAMA

You don't really know what you will do in retirement until you retire. And even then, retirement tends to be an unfolding drama. A corporate colleague of mine—I'll call him John—retired with a basic twofold plan: to write and to play golf for all of his retirement years. Alternating writing and golfing worked out pretty well for two or three retirement years. Then John said he had written everything he had to write and was frankly tired of playing golf with the same group every week.

Phase one of retirement had been a nice blend of work and play for him. But he no longer felt productive or challenged, and he wasn't enjoying retirement to the degree he had planned. So John accepted a church's call to become their interim pastor, which in time changed to a call to be their full-time pastor.

In the unfolding will of God, both John and his wife found new joy in a new challenge. Actually it was an old challenge renewed. Before a career in denominational church work at a national level, he had been a pastor. After those early careers and his first retirement, John is much wiser and more experienced as a pastor in yet another chapter of life. His first retirement plan panned out all right for a while, but then he needed a mini-sabbatical from it. Then he went back to work. Further, John's wife seems to be finding happiness and fulfillment in her own work, which is different from John's but complements his calling.

Although I don't golf, many of my friends seem to have chosen golf as one of their favorite retirement activities. Jim Clark told me he had planned to play golf daily when he retired. After several years in retirement, he told me he played golf only occasionally. He confessed to me that in his preretirement years he hadn't fully prepared for a retirement lifestyle. But from my own knowledge, I've seen Jim accept the developmental task of how to be a good steward of his retirement time and how to have a productive retirement.

In Jim's first minichapter of retirement, he did contract work for a publishers association for a few years, which made good use of career skills that were sharply honed and very helpful on an interim basis. In another minichapter of retirement, Jim did bookkeeping work and hands-on construction with Habitat for Humanity. He and his wife, Flo, paired up as a team in the Habitat efforts.

Next, Jim got specialized training to help people with their tax returns and did seasonal work for the Internal Revenue Service to help average citizens who needed income tax filing help. Because of earlier earnings tests of Social Security for retirees, Jim made just a pittance for his different labors, but he did each of them more for a ministry than for the money.

So after having entered retirement but not fully prepared for it, Jim further prepared himself and continued to move on with good health and productivity in a meaningful retirement. All of the retirement work I've mentioned was in addition to other time spent with children, grandchildren, and caring for elderly in-laws' needs for transportation, counsel, and guidance.

What you have just read are examples to suggest that retirement is not one-dimensional. It has both the potential and the likelihood of being as varied and multifaceted as the first part of life has been—and perhaps even more so.

Up to retirement, what people do with their lives varies greatly, and that variety will continue on into retirement despite the fact that they all are referred to as *seniors* or *retirees*. But none of us reaches retirement age without having had chosen experiences, unchosen experiences, ups and downs, griefs and gladnesses, goals reached and unreached. In other words, up to retirement, life has been anything but uniform or one-dimensional. So why should anyone plan and think that their retirement will be lived on a plane without mountains and valleys? And why should retirement plans ever get limited only to what we can think of before we retire? Chances are that the searching retiree will find the retirement chapter of life to be an unfolding drama filled with serendipities.

Just in case you're not familiar with serendipities, I'll say a word about them. *Serendip* is the ancient Arabian name for Sri Lanka or Ceylon, the Asian island nation. A fairy tale is told of King Fafer of Serendip sending his three prince sons out to broaden their education. The three princes were always searching for one thing but finding something else—a serendipity—which was better than what they had originally hoped to find. These accidental "happies" of life do not come to the idle but to those who are actively involved in life and pursuing goals or dreams that seem right for them. In my case, I've found God's serendipities to be far better than my best-laid plans. Downsized? No, I'm right-sized with quality.

A DRAMA REWRITTEN

During the youth years of our marriage, Phyllis and I were volunteers to be career missionaries. After years of schooling and hard work to pay down our debts, we had finally jumped through all the formal hoops of our denomination's foreign-mission board and were ready for appointment as missionaries to Asia. But at the last stage of getting physical and psychiatric checks, we got a medical rejection. Now I can laugh when I look back and say that I don't know whether the medical rejection was physical or psychiatric. But at the time, we were grieved that our unfolding drama seemed to fold up before ever getting the chance to open. Had we misunderstood God's will? What was *Deo volente*—God's will?

With our first sense of calling and personal choice gone, we did the best we could with second choices. With the healing of time and the arrival of other opportunities, we began to make other first choices that seemed to be God's will for us. To compress career years into a sentence, here's what I did for about thirty years: In sequence, I pastored a church, wrote Bible study curriculum materials, accepted an invitation to become an editor of curriculum materials, and then had six different positions in the publishing house over the next twenty-two years. Those career years were rich and fulfilling, but we never lost sight of our commitment to missions even while we were ministering in other ways.

As homemaker Phyllis and I dreamed and talked about retirement, we envisioned that I might retire at sixty-two, or not later than sixty-five, and then we would do retirement together. Besides common retirement thoughts about travel, writing, sports, hiking, and time with family, we both felt we might be able to do some volunteer mission work—as we had first felt called to do.

But that kind of retirement still seemed distant when it suddenly became present tense at age fifty-five. Although the fact of early, forced retirement seemed like a disaster, it was just an open door to the unfolding drama of God's will for us. The overnight retirement opened the way to our retirement dreams, but so far retirement has been far richer than we could ever have planned by ourselves. What might have been only black and white has been as colorful as a rainbow.

With friend Chuck Morris's counsel of "just don't leave it unwritten" ringing within us, we didn't hesitate to take a sabbatical. We had worked hard all our lives, been productive, raised our boys to adulthood, and were now at a crossroads. So we paused from work for rest and to discover God's will for the next chapter of life. You've already read about the sabbatical, so now I'll tell you how our calling has continued in retirement, which has implications for you.

RETIREMENT SERENDIPITIES

Near the front end of my first retirement, a struggling church asked me to be their interim pastor and help keep them afloat until they could call a "real" pastor. I did, and they did. Phyllis and I found joy in returning to a small church that had a big heart and big dreams. And in the midst of that work, a publisher asked me to do some contract consulting related to a Bible translation. Also, about that time, I began writing a weekly column titled "Words and Things" for our local newspaper. Besides choosing one English word's etymology and meaning to write on each week, I wrote the "things" part about whatever my heart chose. I wrote in people-talk instead of stained-glass language but often bootlegged gospel into the secular newspaper, which got into the everyday world of schools, homes, and businesses. I wrote that column for nine years.

As retirement moved on in its stages, I got a call from the president of a Christian publishers association. On behalf of the association, he asked me to head up a publishers exhibit and delegation to the International Book Fair in Beijing, China. He also invited me to contract with the association to head up an effort to promote indigenous publishing abroad as a mission outreach of the Christian publishers association. We were to help Christian nationals learn to do their own publishing and marketing. Phyllis would be my colaborer in the work.

It seemed to be the will of God, so we accepted the invitations. Can you imagine how we felt as we crossed the Pacific to be missionaries to Asia in a far wider role than we had dreamed of over thirty years earlier? Can you imagine the feeling we had of being free to display open Bibles in Beijing, China, which is the capital of the largest Communist country left in the world today?

Further, a significant part of our work was to partner with and help equip Hong Kong Christian publishers to be prepared for the July 1, 1997, handover of Hong Kong to the People's Republic of China. In that work, Phyllis and I found a home and a family among the many Christian publishers in Hong Kong. Even after our contract work was over, we felt we had left our heart in Hong Kong. We still counsel and encourage the Christian publishers there as they faithfully respond to God's will and also serve as good citizens of their country.

About our first sense of calling, personal choice, and puzzlement over God's will, we had everything right except God's timetable! When our minds and hearts were ready to become missionaries, we didn't know it, but we weren't fully prepared and experienced for what God wanted us to do over thirty years later.

The indigenous Christian publishing outreach also led us to Europe and partnership work with others there. We mostly participated in and partially funded seminars to train leaders in new Christian publishing houses that had sprung up in countries where Communism had fallen. So once again we had the feeling of being missionaries to help spread the gospel where Communism had shown failures in atheism and economy.

Before our second trip to the Beijing International Book Fair, a nearby church asked me to be interim pastor. The church's call seemed to mesh God's will and our good feelings about a church during its pastoral transition time. But we were headed to China. The church said it would gladly wait until we got back from the China mission. So when we returned home, we accepted the church's invitation and concluded our formal work—but not our informal work—of promoting indigenous Christian publishing abroad. So we began another retirement.

The church was relatively small, but it was the largest church in a county-seat town. Its history was rich, and its heritage was grand. But in recent years, for a number of reasons, the church had experienced difficulty in matching up with a pastor who would come and stay for more than a year or two. I didn't ask anything about the past but preached for fourteen months about the unity and harmony required for a people to become the kind of church God wants a church to be.

At that church—as well as in other interims—Phyllis was my uncalled, unpaid, but effective minister of outreach. We loved going to the church and its field on Sundays and Wednesdays. Every Sunday morning, I would get up to preach and say in all honesty, "I would rather be here this morning than any other place in the world." The church wanted to call me as pastor, but I didn't feel that was God's will. And sure enough, God led them in unity to call a younger Timothy instead of an older Paul. Now, some years later, the church is doing well under the mature leadership of a fine pastor.

Soon after the interim pastorate ended, I got a call from a Christian publisher in Birmingham, Alabama, to ask me if I had anyone to recommend as the director for their newly formed general trade division. I had spent most of my career in that work and did have a few names to suggest, so I gave my suggestions. After a couple of months had gone by, I got another call to say that for one reason or another those people I had suggested hadn't quite been a match for the position. Were there any others I could recommend?

Time at the publishing house was critical because of so many things in motion that called for experience and direction. When I couldn't think of any other names to recommend, I left a message that I might be available as interim director for a few months. The reply was immediate that such a working relationship was an answer to prayer. And for over three months, I got to use some skills I hadn't had the chance to use since I retired.

It was also a chance for me to mentor several already-skilled professionals who were nevertheless new to general trade publishing and needed help. Further, I was able to work with the publishing house CEO to interview candidates to become the ongoing director. And I stayed for the time necessary to bridge the gap until a full-time director came on board. Since then, I've served as consultant to that publishing house after a change of administration and because of growing needs during a new millennium.

All of these serendipities were grander than I could have imagined or dreamed up on my own. But now it was time for a minisabbatical.

A Minisabbatical

After Phyllis's early marriage years of heavy church responsibilities as a pastor's wife, my change to publishing and our move to Tennessee caused her to miss the church ministry role she had loved and become accustomed to. As a pastor, I had been in and out of home during the day. But as an editor, I was now gone from dark in the morning until dark at night. So besides

Phyllis's priorities of being wife and mother, she felt the need to minister in other ways in our then-new community.

For the better part of all my career years, Phyllis has had her own calling as well as the ones we've shared. She established a nursing home ministry in 1971 that she still leads along with some other women. She began to teach English as a second language (ESL) to internationals and has done friendship evangelism for many years right here in our own area. In 1993 Phyllis went to Japan for two weeks as a part of our sister-city relationship with Tsuru in the Yamanashi Prefecture. When she came back, she was so excited and bubbling over that she told me she wanted me to go back with her when I could.

And, in time, we decided to take a minisabbatical by visiting her former students and their families in Japan. I made the air travel plans. Phyllis wrote twenty-two of her former students and told them we would be in their area for a couple of weeks and would enjoy visiting with them. We enlisted friend and former student Yumiko Komiya to be our contact person. She speaks excellent English and had only recently returned with her husband, Shinji, from living in our area, where he worked for a few years.

In just a few short weeks after the letters went out from us, Yumiko e-mailed that there were more families wanting us to stay with them than we had days in Japan. We were hosted like royalty and accepted as family in Japanese homes for all of our nights and days there. We found opportunities to answer questions about what it means to be born again, to take a non-Christian couple to visit an evangelical church with us, and also to model the Christian life in a way that we hope will bear evangelistic results. What a serendipity for Phyllis to involve me in her ministry! If you will recall our first sense of calling to Asia, you might now smile with us about God's providence in this minisabbatical trip to Japan. God chooses to reveal His designs one step at a time for most of us. But we can be sure that there is a divine paradigm.

THE DIVINE PARADIGM

Besides everything I've told you so far, I'm still writing the retirement chapter of life. Since that chapter isn't finished, I don't know how it will turn out. I do know that the indispensable ingredient in a productive retirement for Phyllis and me is *Deo volente*. We still can't see around the corner, but we're still following the blueprint. So far we haven't taken any dead-end streets. We have both experience and confidence that God's paradigm is divine. So we want to follow it.

And I recommend that you also look to God's divine paradigm as a foundation for writing your retirement chapter. This chapter itself is made up of minichapters. Regardless of your age or stage in life and despite the fact you can't see your way to the end of the book, you will be wise to start writing on the basis of what you can know and can see. God will then reveal the next steps.

If you have a sense of divine calling, you will find that retirement is not a dead end but an interlude. It is not a retreat or defeat—even if you retire against your own personal choice—but a rest for further meaningful and productive living. It is time to retool, reequip, reorganize, and refocus life. It's time to write life's next chapter. And it's critical that you not leave it unwritten.

Reflections and Projections

- What are some first choices you didn't get?
- Try to identify a second choice that turned out better than your first one likely would have.
- Consider retirement priorities you've decided on or are thinking about; then reconsider and perhaps reorder those priorities in line with what you believe is God's will for you in this chapter of life.
- Consider the possibility of returning to at least one of your first choices.
- As you continue your Christian calling, what are some options that might especially fit under the heading *Deo volente*?
- To begin writing life's retirement chapter, decide on at least one worthy goal that requires plans, actions, and a completion date. Then begin by putting your decision in writing and sharing it with at least one other person. Keep your written goals before you daily until they're reached.

Retirement Words from the Word

Philippians 3:14; Romans 12:2; Ephesians 4:1; James 4:15

Prayer Thoughts

Father, You are the Author and Finisher of my faith, which includes all of life. As I write this retirement chapter, may I look to You both for its content and how best to go about writing it. I pray You will enable the desires of my heart; but if those desires are not within Your design, not my will but Thine be done. Amen.

CHAPTER FOUR

UNMATCHED MATES?

Marriage is that relation between man and woman
in which the independence is equal,
the dependence mutual,
and the obligation reciprocal.

LOUIS K. ANSPACHER

Phyllis and I were never single adults because we were both so young that we had to get our parents to sign for us when we got our marriage license. As the saying goes, "They said we were too young," and they were right. I was barely nineteen, and Phyllis was still seventeen. Nevertheless, both of us are still glad we met, matched up, married, and became mates when we did. Our years together have been rich enough to be called golden even before we reach that fifty-year marker.

Though we were pretty much a perfect match when we became mates, since then we've sometimes been mismatched in wants, likes, dislikes, attitudes, and so forth. But our marriage is still alive and growing in love and friendship and the joy of sharing life together. Now, without any qualifiers on what I've just told you, I have to honestly say that retirement tends to cause husbands and wives to discover ways they've become un-matched mates.

An Oxymoron?

By definition, a *mate* is "a match." So to speak of unmatched mates seems to be an oxymoron—a contradiction in terms. But the term *unmatched mates* applies in one way or another to most marriages when mates retire. The radical changes in their rela-tionship at retirement may require more adjustments than were necessary even in the first year of marriage. In retirement, there is a critical need for mates to rematch and mesh with each other if they are to make the most of their retirement years.

Although we live under the divine imperative of God's call-ing, we live with and among human beings. If we're married, we live most closely with another who is one flesh with us—our other self, our counterpart, our helpmeet. And retirement spells crisis for this relationship. Not disaster, but crisis—which means a time for judgment, change, decision-making, and synchroniz-ing. A checkup on how well mates match up at retirement can avoid marital disharmony and a lot of unnecessary conflict.

Clichés, Commitments, and Plans

One humorous—but serious—retirement cliché goes like this: "I married him for better or worse but not for lunch." Another cliché says "I've got twice as much husband on half as much money." Over the years, I've performed many marriages, and what I said during each ceremony was about the least important thing of the event to the couple getting married. They wanted to get the words over with and get on with marriage. And the words of the vows weren't really as important as the fact of commitment. But retirement time calls to mind once again the marriage vows even if the remembrance is stated humorously.

The unwritten vows of marriage come out in retirement. Marriage ceremonies usually just state the bare facts and intent of marriage in outline form. The details and subpoints come after that throughout all the seasons of marriage. As Ruby Dee said in *I Dream a World*, "One marries many times at many levels within a marriage." In *The Second Neurotic's Notebook*, Mignon McLaughlin wrote, "A successful marriage requires falling in love many times, always with the same person." Andre Maurois put it this way: "A successful marriage is an edifice that must be rebuilt every day." A priority retirement task calls for married couples to clarify, recommit, and match up again in marriage.

Psychotherapist Betty Polston said, "Everyone has a financial plan for retirement, and a health plan; no one bothers to make a relationship plan" (*Time*, November 22, 1999). Retirement does not come in one size or pattern for all. Singles retire; husbands retire; two-income couples retire even if at separate times; and circumstances are varied and complex. But it's wise counsel for everyone to work on a relationship plan as they approach retirement—or to work on one even if they're already in retirement. That's why we're looking at clichés, commitments, and plans.

REMARRYING FOR LUNCH

When the retirement season of marriage comes, it's a good time to remarry for lunch. Now, I don't mean that the wife should fix lunch every day for the retired husband—or vice versa. Rather, I'm using *remarrying for lunch* symbolically to refer to the unwritten or unspoken marriage agreements and understandings that need a little WD-40 in retirement. The lubrication of retirement for mates is good communication and happy understandings. So let's just look at lunch as an illustration of the bigger picture.

When I was involuntarily retired, suddenly I was at home for lunch as well as for breakfast and dinner. But I told Phyllis at the very beginning that I didn't want her to change any of her enjoyable life patterns or routines just because I was retired. Specifically, I said, "Don't worry about lunch for me." And she took me at my word.

Still, she usually invites me to share a sandwich, a salad, or soup with her if we're both home at lunchtime. Often though, she also communicates a coded message we both understand. She says, "I'm just going to eat some fruit for lunch." That's her way of saying to me, "You're on your own. I'm not going to fix a sandwich, a salad, soup, or anything else." That's just fine with me. And I make do. Why, I myself have even eaten fruit for lunch on rare occasions. And on even rarer occasions, I've opened a can of soup and heated it for both of us. The critical thing here is that we have a happy agreement about meals, and we communicate clearly to let each other know what to expect.

UNMATCHED COMMUNICATION

In retirement, unmatched communication between mates can cause them more trouble than most anything else. This problem may get worse instead of better if mates are on different wavelengths, give unclear signals, fail to clear up ambiguities, or make wrong assumptions. It's better to risk overcommunicating to be clear than to undercommunicate and be misunderstood.

That brings up another mismatch that often has occurred between early romance and retirement. In courtship days, infatuated couples talk like magpies and listen to each other intently because they want to know all about each other. They're interested in each other. But in retirement, mates may find they're unmatched in communication.

For example, a newly retired person was probably used to being listened to in the workplace. But upon retirement and at home, he may not be listened to and may bristle over frequent interruptions. However, consider the homemaker's situation. She hasn't had someone at home all the time to talk to or listen to. So when the new invader of her day space starts talking, she may not realize she's interrupting him, because she wasn't listening in the first place.

It has been said that the first duty of love is to listen. Interrupting a mate guarantees broken communication and often downsizes any interest in communicating. On the other hand, a mate ought not talk so much that he or she needs to be interrupted. This kind of problem works both ways. In other words, it's not gender specific, and either one may be the talker or the nonlistener or the interrupter. Either way, the failure to pay attention and focus on each other's communication calls for attention in retirement.

Balance and sensitivity are important in tolerating mere repetition and in being alert for what may be new information. Mates may think they know all about each other, but they don't: Each one is always becoming and has new pages and chapters in the book that has yet to be written.

Further, the very fact that mates have been married for decades often leads each of them to expect the other to fully understand a grunt, a look, or a context that is only hinted at. If so, it's time to go back to the good courtship habit of face-to-face eye contact and listening until understanding takes place.

When we don't understand each other, reading between the lines of communication may sometimes be helpful. At other times, we read between the lines what is not there and come up with bad assumptions or bad conclusions. So it's good to be charitable and to give the benefit of the doubt in all retired-mate communications.

Finally, the simple physical mechanics of communication tend to go downhill as we get older. I consider myself to be a pretty fair public speaker, but around the house, I've noticed I'm often guilty of mumbling and not facing Phyllis when I speak to her. Sometimes when I speak, Phyllis has to be facing me and also able to read lips to understand what I'm saying. Well, I'm trying to improve on this matter.

On the other hand, Phyllis doesn't hear as well as she used to. One bright morning I woke her up by saying in a full voice, "Good morning, sugar plum."

She groggily said, "Did you say someone's on the phone?"

I repeated my greeting. Though it was early and we were still sleepy, we've had a lot of these kinds of conversations when both of us were fully awake and conscious. So I sometimes just say, "Mumble, mumble, mumble."

Then she says, "What did you say, darling?" And then I go ahead and tell her what I would otherwise have had to repeat if I hadn't first said, "Mumble, mumble, mumble."

When we're being our best retired selves, we just laugh and say, "We're a pair, aren't we?" That kind of thing helps us to keep on being a team. But when I'm not being my best self, the atmosphere isn't that pleasant. If communication efforts become too difficult for one or both mates, the efforts may cease, and an unwelcome silence may take its place. So working on communication is definitely a biggie for retirement.

OCCUPYING THE SAME SPACE

Disagreements, arguments, and moodiness are a part of most honest marriages. But the collisions tend to occur with more frequency in retirement when both mates occupy the same space all the time. Before retirement, mates typically have shared the same space overnight and part of each day. But during the day, they have gone their separate ways: one at home and one at the office, both away at work, or some other pattern of not occupying the same space.

Retirement brings the mates together in the same space in a way that can be claustrophobic—no matter how big the house is. Obviously, the matter of space is not only a literal reference to home, even though that is a big part of it. There is a phenomenon best illustrated through the testimonies of some of those who have retired.

The wife of a couple who are friends of ours queried folks on an Internet bulletin board about how to adjust to retirement with her husband. She wrote, "Well, the husband is retiring.

I've been at home pretty much alone for years and years. I have my own life. What do we do? How do we face life together in this house twenty-four hours a day?" The homemaking woman felt she had lost her house when her husband retired. She felt the need to reestablish her territory in her own home—which was, of course, also the husband's home.

Further, she had had her own car and given up that feeling of independence and private space when she and her husband decided to downsize to one car. So she felt she had lost her home, her car, her independence, her place, and her space. The husband had his own losses, of course, but he wasn't the one writing on the Internet bulletin board for counsel, so I'll focus on husbands later.

The males' replies to the wife's Internet questions tended to be lighthearted and to pooh-pooh the radical effects of retirement on marriage. But both the women homemakers and the women who worked outside the home gave thoughtful replies. One woman wrote, "The shock of retirement will impact you both equally but in different ways. Your space has been invaded, but he's been kicked out of his!"

Another woman told how she and her husband knew about the built-in conflicts they would face because they were so different in nature and liked so many conflicting things. So they laughingly drew up a postretirement contract of what they would expect from each other and agree to. The wife summarized it this way: "We kinda did this as a joke, but it forced us to look at the need for each other to have our own space." Then she went on to tell how great their together time and their apart time is and how they're enjoying retirement.

I suppose all the solutions suggested involve about four major points: (1) Don't get too grim about retirement, and keep on loving each other; (2) give each other time and space alone; (3) find out how you most enjoy being together and spend time that way; and (4) communicate often and on the same wavelength.

An Unwanted Shadow

Part of the problem that relates to space is the feeling that everything is a duet now; there's no such thing as a solo part. There may not be a collision; rather, the mate who used to have a home-and-sashay routine by herself now has an unwanted shadow. One wife wrote that she couldn't even go into the kitchen without her mate following her. The kitchen was narrow, and the husband seemed to want to do his kitchen chores at exactly the same time she chose to do hers. Then when she wanted to shop or run an errand, the shadow was sure to want to go along, too. Her mate matched her moves so closely that he was with her at every turn, and he wanted to help even when she didn't want any help. This match was so close that it didn't fit. Instead of having a mate, she felt more like she had a conjoined twin. The wife needed to breathe on her own and have the solitude that makes the heart grow fonder and gladder upon rejoining one's mate.

From the husband's perspective, he was just doing what he had planned to do in retirement: spend more time with his wife. Also, he wanted to be a help. That's why he offered so many "helpful" suggestions when she started to rearrange the furniture, put up a picture, or make other home choices she had freely made alone through all their married years. The wife's well-meaning feedback to her new retiree husband tended to result in hurt feelings or sad statements such as, "I can't do anything right anymore." Obviously, there was a mismatch in the mates' retirement needs that called for some loving communication about how to get their retirement lives in sync.

REVERSED ROLES

One husband who retired early wrote with a smiley face attached, "It took me six months to drive my wife out of the house. I critiqued everything she was doing while looking over her shoulder. . . . Finally, she took a full-time job and left me home to do my thing." The retired husband went on to describe how he enjoyed taking over most of the things his wife had been doing, and she found that she liked working outside the home. From his report, he and his wife are enjoying both their time together and their time apart as much as ever. He counseled, "If you don't allow each other some space, you can suffocate your relationship."

This husband had come straight out of the business world and appointed himself to be his wife's one-minute manager. His constant performance reviews of her behavior were obviously more than she could take all day every day at home. So she made a choice that seemingly helped her, her husband, and their marriage.

Herbert Samuel wrote, "It takes two to make a marriage a success and only one to make it a failure." No doubt, this statement is true; but it is equally true that one person in a marriage can take the lead in rescuing a sick marriage. And in retirement, this fact especially needs underlining. One positive, kind, loving peacemaker can't cure all the conflicts in a marriage, but the person's attitude and leadership may make the conflicts manageable.

DEALING WITH CONFLICTS

In Jimmy Carter's book *The Virtues of Aging*, he told how he and Rosalynn retired back in Plains, Georgia, and began to deal with the almost inevitable conflicts that come when mates share so much time and space together. He said they arrived at a process that seems to suit both of them pretty well. Sometimes they just talk and iron out a disagreement. Other times, they take a recess and give the argument a rest. Then when they cool off and discuss it again, they tend to calmly and rationally resolve the matter. He did point out that they both had come to realize there were some points of disagreement that simply weren't going to be resolved; they had learned it was best not to go there again. This pattern for dealing with conflicts seems worthy of consideration.

Phyllis and I have probably subconsciously followed pretty much the same pattern as the Carters have in dealing with disagreements. However, I would add that the friendship factor is most important in resolving conflicts. If we're feeling friendly toward each other, most anything we say sails by smoothly. If we're not feeling friendly toward each other, nothing much gets by without some offense being taken. So we try to avoid letting the cause of conflict get deeper than our commitment to friendship.

We've learned to drop seeds of thought that might or might not cause conflict and leave them alone until they've had time to germinate and grow a while. Phyllis is better at this than I am. When the seed is sown, time has passed, and the fruit begins to ripen, she knows how to move in for the harvest. And I might add that this approach allows for a happy harvest that comes in a timely way—not too soon nor too late but when agreement is exactly ripe. Other times we recognize that our disagreement is one of mood, attitude, tiredness, or bad timing. So we talk helpfully about when to do things or when to reconsider them.

Whatever the cause of conflict, it's good to remember to apply the wisdom of Langdon Mitchell from *The New York Idea*: "Marriage is three parts love and seven parts forgiveness."

UNMATCHED MEMORIES

Especially in retirement, mates are wise if they learn not to remember anything with authority. Nothing conflicts like memories. Mates who want to avoid disagreements over memories soon learn to use caution. They check with each other before they are specific about dates, places, events, names, or anything else when they're talking to others.

Some couples become experts at padding whatever they tell. One will get ready to state a date but pause and ask, "What year was that, dear?" Or, at the beginning, the padding may go this way: John says, "I'll have to ask Mary to help me with the facts on this story." We grow accustomed to interruptions and corrections. That doesn't mean we like it or appreciate it. That's just the way it is.

The classic statement of unmatched memories came from *Gigi* when Maurice Chevalier sang, "I Remember It Well." Everything he remembered well was wrong—at least, according to his mate.

What would it hurt if we allowed our mates to go right on with a story and miss half the details? We might even smile and nod with enjoyment as the mate tells the story. That could put an end to halting speech, nervous eyes, and tentative statements. Further, such gentle silence or positive body language might reinvent the joy of seeing one's mate enjoy telling stories, events, and memories. Of course, if it's a matter of life and death or grave danger, that's a matter worth correcting or questioning.

Proving that your memory is correct and that your mate's memory is wrong is a lose-lose situation. Now, I've kept a daily diary since I was sixteen years old. And it is true that the dimmest ink is stronger than the strongest memory. But whenever I've pulled out a diary to prove that I'm right on a memory, I've already lost by offending my Phyllis. And from time to time, my diary proves that my memory was wrong, so I lose again. We've improved on sharing dates about events by agreeing to just say *many years ago*, which means neither of us remembers exactly when it was.

The compulsion to prove you're right may grow strong in retirement. Arguments may occur over things small, medium, or large. In most things, it's probably better not to worry about who's right. It tends to be a lose-lose situation that injures the marriage and other relationships. As a rule, it's better to be loving and forgiving and uncertain about memories than to be right. As Christina Rossetti said, "Better by far you should forget and smile, than that you should remember and be sad" (*Say It Again*).

MATES MATCHED

Ideally, mates are matched in retirement by a voluntary, mutual submission that places a foundation under each other. The Bible says, "Submit to one another out of reverence for Christ" (Ephesians 5:21 NIV). Although the Bible states that the husband is to be the spiritual leader and head of the home, the focus is on mutual love and respect that puts each other first. The Greek word for *submit* in Ephesians 5:21 is *hupotassomai*, and it literally means *to place under*. I heard a scholar once say that the word was used in ancient times to talk about placing a foundation under something. Regardless of word meanings, the right matching for husband and wife in all of life and especially in retirement is to place a foundation under each other—instead of knocking out the props.

I agree with Pearl Buck, who said, "Nothing in life is as good as the marriage of true minds between man and woman. As good? It is life itself" (*To My Daughters, with Love*). I agree with Aeschylus, who said, "When a match has equal partners, then I fear not." And in essence, Henry Ward Beecher said, "Well-married, a person is winged; ill-matched, he is shackled."

Whatever retirement holds for a husband and wife, it is a grand chapter in life that they have the opportunity to write together. And part of the adventure is learning how to match each other's lives as complements and as helpmeets. As good stewards, our job is to return our mate to God better than when we first married. So match up, and write that chapter especially well.

REFLECTIONS AND PROJECTIONS

- When you first married, in what ways were you matched and unmatched?
- Separately from your mate, identify in two columns how you feel you and your mate are most matched and most un-matched now.
- For both mates: Swap your matched-and-unmatched lists with your mate for study without comment.
- For both mates: Without agreeing or disagreeing on items listed, choose one item that each of you will happily agree to try to match the other's expectations on.
- Out of a personal want-to, choose some special way you will try to place a retirement foundation under your mate—for example, an attitude, an act, a new habit, showing renewed love and respect, or giving up something that you know irri-tates your mate.

RETIREMENT WORDS FROM THE WORD
Ephesians 5:33; 1 Peter 3:7; Proverbs 5:17; Proverbs 19:14

PRAYER THOUGHTS
Father, I give thanks that You yoked our lives together in marriage. Help us at this stage of life to be sensitive to ways that we pull against each other. And I pray that You will once again match our lives in all the ways that will please You and be a blessing for us and for others. Amen.

CHAPTER FIVE

WHY RETIRED MEN ARE HARD TO LIVE WITH

Being a woman is a terribly difficult task,
since it consists principally in dealing with men.

JOSEPH CONRAD

I wrote all chapters of this book for both genders. However, this chapter and the next one attempt to look objectively at some gender-specific traits with the intent of helping both husbands and wives in retirement. Wives will realize that this chapter is only summary and that the subject really calls for a book of its own.

Men may feel that there should be another chapter in this book titled "Why Retired Women Are Hard to Live With." Could be. However, although the context of this chapter is gender specific, much of it would apply equally well to those of either sex who retire and join a mate at home. And examples I give of both male and female tendencies may be just the reverse in any given situation. Regardless of gender, the purpose of this chapter is to help mates better understand each other and have a happy retirement relationship.

THE AGENDA QUESTION

On my first full day of retirement, Phyllis innocently asked, "What's on your agenda for today?" For some reason, that question caused me to flare up, and I replied tensely and tersely, "I don't have an agenda for the day." And what's more, I didn't want one. I had had an agenda for almost every day of my working life. To me, retirement meant not having an agenda.

But in reflection, I wondered—as did Phyllis—why her simple question drew an emotional response from me. Later, she explained that she had merely wanted to know whether she was included in my plans for the day and how she might prepare to adjust her own schedule to mesh with mine. So her intent had been good.

Perhaps I had thought there was an ulterior motive to the question—prepping me for my first retirement honey-do list. Perhaps a lifetime of full agendas had suggested pressure to perform to someone else's standards, and *that* bothered me. Whatever the reason for my response, Phyllis put the agenda question in her don't-ask-him box. Incidentally, some months later she did put a small list on the fridge that she titled HONEY, PLEASE LIST, and she never mentioned it. But I found myself wanting to do those things to please her.

In social gatherings with retiree friends and their spouses, I learned the agenda question is a standard one that spouses of recent retirees ask. I also learned that the wives were at a total loss to explain why the husbands blew up over such a simple question.

Now that I've been retired several years, the agenda question is no big deal. In fact, I enjoy pulling out my to-do list and sharing it (see the later chapter on "Ruts and Routines"). But it took time to get to that point. That first husband-wife retirement encounter was just a hint of some hard adjustment times ahead. It also signaled that this male retiree would be a challenge to live with.

Many retirement households are like a minefield with explosions waiting to take place. If a wife is aware of and sensitive to where the mines are, she can avoid them, deal with them, or work around them. To help with that awareness and sensitivity, I'm willing to bear down on why retired men are hard to live with. Well, they're not always hard to live with, but frequently they are. So let's take a look at where some of the mines are and why retired men are hard to live with.

BECAUSE THEY'RE MEN

Basically, retired men are hard to live with because of who they are, how they feel, what they think, and how they behave. I'm not writing to defend retired men and what makes them hard to get along with but, rather, to give insight and offer a few suggestions that might be helpful.

Retired men are hard to live with because they're men. No matter what you or I think about political correctness, inclusive language, or equality of the sexes, the fact remains that men and women are different. The stereotypes of genders may not be correct and may only satirize male and female traits. But without being rigid or sexist, most of us recognize some gender differences besides physical sexual characteristics.

For example, my sister Marylyn and I machine-gun e-mails back and forth daily. But occasionally Phyllis will e-mail Marylyn. When that happened one time, Marylyn noted with delight how glad she was to get Phyllis's different kind of content and perspective. When I asked Marylyn specifically what the difference was between my e-mails and those of Phyllis's, this is how she answered: "You tend to write in outline; Phyllis fills in the details."

Just a few days after that, I happened upon a televised marriage enrichment seminar in which the male leader said, "Women want all the details; men just give the summary facts." Now, if the subject is sports, cars, computers, or investments, men may put in endless details; but on matters of the heart and caring, I suppose it's fair to say we men tend to speak in outline.

What I've just told you doesn't necessarily make retired men hard to live with, but it does reflect a different approach to communication and some other differences. To illustrate that, I know one man who doesn't use a whole lot of words to tell what he wants to say while his wife could win the flaming-tongue award. And when she's in the midst of a war of words, he sometimes says to me, "Who cares?" And his wife sometimes finds him hard to live with.

FROM SOMEBODY TO HAS-BEEN

Ask a retired man who he is, and chances are, he'll tell you who he has been. Usually, he does that by telling you about the work that defined his life and gave meaning to it—what he has done and what he has been. He feels that there's nothing else to add to his resume, which has been growing through all the years of his life. When the man had a title and a job—no matter how magnificent or how mundane—he knew who he was and knew what he was supposed to do. But now he feels like a has-been.

After several years of my own retirement, I met a jolly fellow who had been retired for twenty-two years, and we got to talking about retirement. He asked me how long I had been retired and which retirement I was in. Then he explained that he takes aside guys who are getting ready to retire and enlightens them about what they're going to face. Here's what he tells them: "As you begin your first retirement, you'll find that you are the dumbest person on earth and that you don't have any authority. You're on Momma's turf." Although he's retired two or three more times after his first retirement, he still holds that same viewpoint.

We're fond of saying a person is who he is and not what he does, but the truth is that our mind doesn't make that distinction. To the man, he was his work, and now he has lost himself. The retiree has to struggle to know who he is in the present tense. He needs to know that he is a somebody, not a nobody. He won't find rest for the frustration of his identity and personhood until he has discovered a new niche for his life—sometimes not until he's retooled and refired.

After the euphoria of retirement is over, the unoccupied man may well tend to grow restless, irritable, unhappy, depressed, or whatever, and become hard to live with. Fortunately, this developmental stage of retirement is a passage that usually passes soon—with patience, time, and the right kind of help from spouse, family, and friends.

DISDAIN FOR THE MUNDANE

When men are good at their work, they're proud of it and their accomplishments. But when what they're good at ends with retirement, they often look at common tasks as beneath their dignity or not deserving of their time and attention. The comedown from career pride is a humbling experience and takes some getting used to. Part of the retirement transition is moving from the meaningful to the menial that a person had little or no time for during a busy career.

For example, before retirement, I used to sign contracts that involved millions of dollars and do business with shakers and movers. There was a zing to the negotiation and contract signing and the interaction with others. My work career had a lot of pizzazz to it. Then came retirement.

When I went back to my former workplace for a brief visit, the veteran security guard at the entrance subconsciously put into words what had happened to me. She was talking with a newly employed maintenance man but happily interrupted her conversation to greet me. Then with all sincerity and no humor or slight intended, she introduced me to the man by saying, "This is Johnnie Godwin. He used to be important." I didn't mind what she said, but it did remind me that I was no longer a corporate cog; I was a corporate has-been.

Further, after Phyllis and I got back from our sabbatical cruise, the grass needed mowing. Since my work career included being gone from dark to dark or being out of town and our boys were grown and gone, I had kept Phyllis in the best yard-cutting equipment money could buy.

But now, in retirement, as I sat on the riding mower, I felt somewhat deflated. The only joy I found in mowing grass was seeing how well I could take corners with the mower revved up to top speed. In fact, my neighbor commented, "You sure do mow fast." And I did.

The garbage needed taking out, and I started doing that. On the way to the garbage can, I remembered that in corporate life someone else had done that every night, and I was never bothered with it. In retirement, I had moved from managing contracts, strategies, goals, missions, visions, and budgets to mowing grass, killing time, doing household chores, going to weddings and funerals, and attending what I called pink-tea affairs. I felt a disdain for the mundane. And, mind you, I'm basically a positive, upbeat person and don't let myself wallow in depression or self-pity. So this letdown feeling was temporary.

Typically, though, it's about this stage in retirement when unasked-for counsel comes from mates, family, friends, and others. As friend John Scott once told me, unasked-for counsel is usually perceived as criticism. And, sure enough, when the retiree gets time on his hands and others suggest ways for him to fill up his time and stay busy, he feels criticized rather than helped. Or he may simply feel pressure to conform to others' suggestions about ways to fill up time.

The retiree doesn't want or need something to fill up his time; rather, he needs his life to be filled up with meaning. His need is not for busyness, but for significance. He has lost his sense of significance and importance. He had a former life and needs to get a new life. So he needs what he himself considers significant activity for his life and the joy that comes with making his own choices.

The retiree no longer has a *have-to*. His *want-to* may be gone also. It's worth repeating that he needs the magnificent compulsion of a new *got-to* that he wants to do. So suggestions about volunteer work, being a greeter at a store, or helping out at the church, chamber of commerce, or hospital may not hold any appeal for him right now.

The retiree may welcome specific invitations he can say yes to with joy or no to without resentment or guilt. But he still has to find and choose retirement life for himself. Otherwise, he'll be an unhappy camper, and he'll make the other campers around him unhappy, too. This agitation may just add the fermentation necessary to produce a new wine in life, which may cause the last to be better than the first. But temporarily, at least, it often makes retired men hard to live with.

MEN TREATED AS BOYS

Regardless of what kind of work and what level of position a person had in his career life, he was entrusted with a job and held accountable for performing it well. Typically, the job required him to drive to work in traffic, be alert to schedules, interact with people of all sorts, make decisions, and use his head as a responsible person. Whether he was supervisor, supervisee, or both, he was treated as an adult and expected to perform with a good degree of maturity and wisdom.

But upon retirement, men often get the feeling they're adults being treated as children—men being treated as boys. They feel smothered with instructions, reminders, and cautions. A guy may have flown all over the world and routinely made his way in rental cars to strange places in large cities. Now he may get directions from his spouse on where to turn on the way to the same church they've gone to forever, how fast or slow to drive, when to buy gas, and what to watch out for. He may feel like a teenager learning to drive and not having a license that permits him to drive without the presence and help of another.

When husbands go out for a doctor's appointment or to get a car serviced, they often find themselves getting counsel like this: "You ought to take something to read so you'll have something to do while you wait." The husband who is going to be outside thirty seconds between his car and his inside destination sometimes hears, "You had better wear a coat, or you'll catch your death of cold." The retiree may feel that his middle name has become *Don't-Forget-To*. The counsel is well meant and probably well deserved, but it tends to stir feelings of *momitis* in the husband—which I define as the "irritation of a wife starting to behave like a mother to her husband"—even though he may need it.

Another *itis* is *correctionitis*. I refer to the irritation of constant correction over nits. Whether it's a question of who did what when and where or whether it's some other kind of fact or sequence of events, it's a good idea to let the nits go. Give them a rest.

Overcoming the urge and impulse to jump in with corrections is worth the effort. It will smooth relations like emotional graphite. Otherwise, the constant correcting can become cumulative like a dripping faucet and wear down the spirit and the relationship. By the way, this counsel is good for all of life and not just for the retirement stage of life. And it applies to both men and women.

EASILY BOTHERED

When author Richard Carlson was speaking to a crowd at a bookstore, one of the people asked him to describe the average person in two words or less. After Carlson thought for a minute, he replied, "Easily bothered" (*Don't Sweat the Small Stuff with your Family*). After I read this question and answer, I gave a good deal of thought to it, and I agree. From my own retirement perspective, I believe "easily bothered" is one of my greatest flaws. And I'm inclined to think we retired men may be hard to live with because we let ourselves become so easily bothered. Many of us lack patience and get grumpy quickly.

My dad was a great guy and lived life and retirement fully until he died at seventy-eight. He took most of life's major trials and tribulations in stride. However, in retirement, he seemed to get especially irritated over little things. I remember my sister telling me that Dad called her one day when he had gotten especially bent out of shape. What was the problem? Well, the delivery schedule for his mail had been in the mornings, but the postal carrier changed the delivery time to the afternoon. Dad's vision had gotten so bad he couldn't see to call the post office. So he was frustrated, mad as a bear, and wanted my sister's help. Most of the mail he got was junk mail, which he couldn't read anyway; but he wanted it delivered early—as it always had been.

Funny thing about that particular matter: Not long ago our own mail delivery changed from morning to late in the afternoon. When I complained to Phyllis about that, she quipped, "Do you want me to ask Marylyn to call the post office and take care of the matter?" We both smiled.

Yep, I'm a chip off the old block; I find myself being more easily bothered than I like to admit. If we run out of ketchup, mustard, or other condiments, I'm upset. If people don't drive down the highway to suit me, I'm bothered. If the green traffic light turns red just as I get to it, that's a frustration.

The same thing could be true for retired women. But somehow it has never frustrated Phyllis to have to stop at a traffic light. And she seldom is bothered about the things I've mentioned that bother me.

Now, I don't want to give the impression that I go around in a bad mood, because I don't. But I do want to confess that I'm too easily bothered. And when I'm easily bothered, that makes me less pleasant to be around part of the time. The same thing is likely true of other retired husbands—and possibly a few wives.

GETTING OVER BEING EASILY BOTHERED

Now, as a rule, most men don't want to be hard to live with. They know when they're being donkeys, but that usually doesn't stop them from braying. And when men get through snorting, kicking and fussing, and being stubborn, they're sorry for their behavior—whether they admit it or not.

If a man has been hard to live with all of his married life, he's probably not going to improve a whole lot in retirement. As Marjorie Kinnan Rawlins wrote, "You can't change a man, no-ways." The late Natalie Wood said, "The only time a woman really succeeds in changing a man is when he's a baby."

On the other hand, if a man has been a decent sort, fairly compatible, and fun to be married to before retirement, that should not go downhill in retirement. So, spouses, there may be hope for retired men who are hard to live with to move to a higher plane of living and get a little more enjoyment out of life. How? I think I have a clue or two.

My sweet mother was not perfect, but she was a saint of a person and knew how to deal with Dad when he got easily bothered. Somehow, in later life, she worked out a code term with him that seemed to work like magic oil on troubled waters when he got upset.

They must have agreed on this thing privately, because neither one of them ever told me about it. But I began to notice that whenever Dad got bothered and in a sour mood, Mother would say, "Now, stay sweet." And Dad would usually back off with quietness—and sometimes with a smile. The man who had been hard to live with suddenly softened to become a kinder and gentler person.

Phyllis was the only one I ever talked to about this change I had noticed in my parents. And I didn't share that matter with her until after I grew a bit unhappy with myself for getting bothered so easily in retirement. When I did share with Phyllis, here's what I told her: "When I get easily bothered or sour, tell me to stay sweet; I'll try to happy up." Now, that might just sound like a gimmick to you, but I want you to know it has worked pretty well for us. I may even have mellowed a little bit.

However hard it is to put up with the ole boy, stay with him. And if you're the ole boy, give yourself a talking to and learn how to stay sweet. Be humble enough to get a little help from your mate. Then the strained, cracked, or broken relationship of married life in retirement can mend instead of destruct. As Cervantes said, "The worst reconciliation is preferable to the best divorce."

It's Mostly Not about Sex

As any wife knows, her retired husband is around the house a lot more than he used to be. In fact, it probably seems like he's always present—except when she needs him. This retirement matter of husband and wife being together so much brings to mind what George Bernard Shaw once said: "Marriage is popular because it combines the maximum of temptation with the maximum of opportunity." Retirement puts that temptation and opportunity together all day most every day. This may mean that the husband wants to do a whole lot more lovemaking than his wife wants to do—regardless of how loving she may be.

Wives need to know that often it's not so much about sex as it is about manhood. A man's feelings of virility can turn to feelings of sterility overnight as he makes the transition from being a productive worker to being a retiree.

If there should be any emotional or physical hint or fact of impotency, the anxiety is compounded. Contemporary humor has expressed it this way: "The difference between the first honeymoon and the retirement honeymoon is the difference between Niagara and Viagra." But it's not really a funny matter, and it may be one of the serious problems that causes a retired man to be unnecessarily hard to live with. Doctors, counselors, and modern therapy and drugs offer more help than ever before—for both sexes—in dealing with intimacy problems, whether the sexual problems are physical, psychological, or both.

Jimmy Carter wrote candidly and helpfully about the sexual relationship in retirement: "Now, well past seventy, Rosalynn and I have learned to accommodate each other's desires more accurately and generously and have never had a more complete and enjoyable relationship" (*The Virtues of Aging*). His comments indicate that dealing with sexuality in retirement is a two-way street and not a male-only concern. Retirement and aging ought never end intimacy and the romance of marriage despite any sexual decline or lessening of ability to perform as well as in earlier years of the marriage.

Jimmy Carter gave further insight into his own feelings about male sexuality and personhood when he shared a moment from a book-signing experience he had. He told how he was signing one of his books at an autograph occasion when an attractive woman in her thirties appeared. She brought a momentary hush to the crowd when she told President Carter that she remembered his *Playboy* interview.

That interview was when Carter's honesty about his humanity had cost him fifteen points in the presidential polls and nearly cost him the election. He admitted that he had lusted after other women and that God had forgiven him. The young woman at the book-signing drew the crowd's laughter and a beet-red face from Carter when she said, "If you still have lust in your heart, I'm available." Carter confessed in his book that, even though he was in his mid-seventies at the time, he enjoyed the encounter. He was glad to know he was still appealing instead of repelling or neutral.

Now, don't get mad at President Carter all over again if you got mad the first time. Rather, get the point. Loving, faithful retirees still love their wives and want to express that love sexually. But more than sexual expression, they want and need to know their manhood and masculine appeal are still intact. Chances are that the wife who goes the second mile in the area of sexual relations with her retired husband will get more dividends than any stock ever paid. And, in time, this facet of retirement life may become more copacetic than it's ever been before.

FOCUS ON MORTALITY

When a man retires, he gets a renewed sense of his mortality. He has time and opportunity to dwell upon the fact that he is only human. He knows that he will have a lot fewer years to live than those already gone by. He'll be going to more funerals for friends of his own age. He'll begin to pay attention to pains that he didn't have time for or didn't notice much when he was working every day. He may develop anxiety symptoms that cloud his daily sunshine with depression. Or, heaven forbid, he may become a hypochondriac who talks about all his aches and pains and unnecessarily goes to the doctor a lot.

Now, there's no denying that the body wears out and expresses its condition through aches and pains. Arthritis comes to live with many of us. Others deal with very real problems of heart disease, cancer, or other diseases. I once read that, after forty, life is just one maintenance problem after another. My corporation's former CEO, Dr. James L. Sullivan, said, "After fifty you hurt somewhere all the time; it just moves around." At my age and stage of life, I agree with both of those opinions. However, it's true that most of us Americans are living longer and healthier lives than ever before.

But our retirement minds may be telling us something to the contrary. And if we feel bad physically or emotionally, we tend to be hard to live with. To paraphrase a cliché, "When poppa doesn't feel good, no one feels good."

Living with an emotionally crippled person is a hard way to go. So it's important to have a healthy perspective on life and death and on pain and feeling good. The most productive retirees refuse to be enslaved to their feelings—whether they're emotional feelings or sensors of physical pain. They come to realize they can do a lot of living between the welcomed retirement and the death they may dread. Retirees need to learn to celebrate the present and not live in chronic wimpism. In the meantime, a wife's patience and care can go a long way to help her mate who is hard to live with.

SUGGESTIONS

I don't have a pat solution or panacea to offer wives who have the hard task of living with retired men. However, I do have a few suggestions, which don't include any walking-on-eggshells approach. Living with retired men doesn't call for timidity but loving confidence expressed with sensitivity, wisdom, and persistence.

Keep a sense of humor. A laugh is better than a frown any day. In fact, I counsel young people to look for a mate who wears a laugh more quickly than a frown. Phyllis's laughter was one of the first things that attracted me to her; even now, her laughter is medicine to my soul and sunshine in our marriage.

Shake it off. Everybody has problems, so don't be a wimp about it. The book of each person's life has good pages and bad pages, but some people choose to dwell on the bad ones. In fact, a wife who claimed she could read her husband like a book may not have been aware that she tended to stop and dwell on the bad pages instead of enjoying the whole book, which wasn't finished yet.

Give it some time. Time doesn't really heal everything, but marriage retirement problems often just need a little time. Then they may disappear or lighten up. The nature and intensity of the problem dictates whether to meet it head-on or to back off for a while and see how things go.

Memorize some appropriate quotes. I love pithy quotations that contain a spot of humor, philosophy, wisdom, or even chagrin. The thoughts of others can help us get perspective on our own lives.

To show you what I'm talking about, here are some samples: "Men can't do anything alone" (Barbara Holland). "There are men I could spend eternity with. But not this life" (Kathleen Norris). When Hermione Gingold was asked if her husband was still living, she replied, "It's a matter of opinion." Henry Kissinger said, "Nobody will ever win the Battle of the Sexes. There's just too much fraternizing with the enemy."

Pray about it. The One who gave you your mate is also the One who can show you how to manage when he's hard to live with. In fact, as P. T. Forsyth once said, "God has some blessings for us we'll never receive unless we ask Him for them." Knowing how to deal with a retired husband who's hard to live with may be one of those blessings that comes as an answer to prayer.

Not all retired men are hard to live with. However, retirement offers new opportunities for relationship collisions between husbands and wives. When the collisions occur, there is a challenge to turn "difficult to live with" into "a joy to live with." Successfully dealing with the challenge is worth the effort. And since I've written out of experience, I'll mention that, after more than a dozen years of my retirement, Phyllis has frequently begun to say, "You sure have mellowed out a lot." I suppose I have in some ways, but I'm aware I haven't arrived yet.

REFLECTIONS AND PROJECTIONS

- What attracted you and led you to marry your mate?
- What has been enjoyable in your marriage up to retirement?
- Identify any major ongoing conflicts within your marriage.
- Recall what the best problem-solving processes in your marriage have been.
- List why you still like and love your mate.
- Identify "mines" to avoid or deal with.
- Plan to use your tried-and-proven problem-solving processes.
- Lovingly suggest a code term to help each other stay sweet.
- Plan regular events you both want to do together.
- Renew your marriage commitment to stay together despite any negative feelings.

RETIREMENT WORDS FROM THE WORD

- Ephesians 4:32;
- "With all humility, gentleness, and patience, put up with one another in love" (Ephesians 4:2, my translation);
- I Peter 3:8;
- "[Love] is not rude, doesn't insist on its own way, isn't easily bothered, and doesn't keep record of wrongs" (I Corinthians 13:5, my translation).

PRAYER THOUGHTS

Father, thank You for giving me a mate. You know my faults and short-comings and still love me and forgive me. You also know that my mate and I sometimes find each other hard to live with in one way or another. So I pray You will help us to keep loving each other and to be as forgiving as You are. Especially help me to be a retired mate who's easier to live with. Amen.

CHAPTER SIX

WHEN WOMEN RETIRE

*Man's superiority will be shown not in the fact
that he has enslaved his wife,
but that he has made her free.*

EUGENE V. DEBS

T he quote you've just read is not intended to be chauvinistic or negative toward women. Rather, the sense of the quote—from the book *Say It Again*, compiled by Dorothy Uris—seems to be this: A husband most nearly rises to his potential in marriage when he helps his wife to be free. Or to put it in my terms, a husband does a super thing when he helps his wife know and share the freedom of retirement. Ideally for couples, retirement is mutual and not exclusively for just one of them. But understanding what retirement means is a key factor here.

Although women who work outside the home retire all the time, it grieves me that there is a sense in which many women homemakers never retire. This chapter speaks to that concern, and I hope it will make a positive difference for husbands and wives who read this book, because women deserve to retire, too.

But we'll start with the status quo of the cliché.

WOMEN NEVER RETIRE

It's almost a truism to hear that women never retire. And it's easy to see why this common statement appears to be true—especially on the surface. When the husband retires, he leaves his work and workplace behind him and appears to be free as a bird. Essentially, there's no work he has to do, no responsibility he has to bear. And his retirement plans tend to look like a holiday every day. He has no boss, no agenda, and luxuriates in his newfound freedom. He is the envy of his homemaking or unretired wife. A cartoon showed a man asleep on the couch while the wife vacuumed and commented, "He's retired, and I'm still just tired."

Take a look at the wife and her situation when the husband retires. She has had her own space and place, her own work routine, and a sense of beginning and ending to projects. Although she's always been subject to emergencies that rearrange her plans, she's usually been able to have her own agenda for the day and work through it with some sense of order and control. Now, with a retired husband at home, things are radically different for the wife.

You already know about "Unmatched Mates" and "Why Retired Men Are Hard to Live With." But chances are that neither the wife nor the husband fully understand the new role the wife finds herself in. She doesn't see that she has one bit less work to do than she had before her husband retired. In fact, she's got more work to do. She's got a husband underfoot most of the time, and he's either in the way of her work or creating more work for her to do or both. When he's not in the way or creating more work, he may be introducing chaos into the orderly routine of his wife and causing her to feel that she has lost control of her own life.

With the impulsiveness of a teenager, the husband's plans may change every fifteen minutes, and he probably wants his wife to be available to fit into those plans. He wants her to go somewhere with him or do something with him. Or he may want to go somewhere or do something alone and hasn't told his mate that he doesn't want a date.

On the other hand, when the wife starts to leave home with her to-do list, her errand-running, or her fun time with the gals she lunches with, her husband may insist on tagging along whether he's wanted or not. His shadow may become a cloud over his wife's existence. Since home is her workplace, she can't easily retire from it as the husband did from his workplace. So, what retirement fun for the wife! She's unretired and already tired of her retired husband.

It doesn't have to be that way. I'll get to that matter in a few minutes. But for now, let's look at what one psychologist has said about the wife's retirement. It's kind of sad, but this stage of life calls both for being realistic and also looking at preferred alternatives to come up with the best one.

A Sad Retirement

Psychologist Paul Tournier wrote that a woman retires when her husband dies and she becomes a widow. How sad—but true in a sense. Once again the woman has control of her life. She can have her own agenda, plan her day, click off her to-do list without a husband's interruption, and have a sense of organization, routine, and closure to projects.

The widow can come and go when she pleases without being shadowed. She has less washing to do and less food to prepare. She can move the furniture around to suit herself without anyone griping about the change. She can go to bed and sleep all night without anyone snoring or tossing and turning to disturb her. She's still got things to do, but mostly she has retired.

I've read enough Ann Landers and Dear Abby columns on this subject to get a sense of prewidowhood and of what many widows feel about that kind of retirement. Typically, the wives who still have their husbands write in with complaints. And before the ink is dry on the published complaints, widows are expressing how they now feel about the matter. Also, I've been the speaker in enough churches, retirement centers, and other high-density centers of widows that I know firsthand how many of them feel after their husband's death.

Most of the widows would gladly exchange their retirement to welcome back a mate despite all his faults. They would love to wash his clothes, cook his meals, feel the warmth of his presence, and even grin over the chagrin of his snoring. They forget or dismiss the small irritations that built up over a lifetime of marriage.

And they yearn for the love and companionship they once had but no longer have. With hindsight, they're able to see that retirement with their mate was a time of shared life on a different plane for both of them than they had known before he retired. Retirement together had offered a chance for the accent on work to shift to the accent on leisure, optional activities, and joint or separate productivity for both of them. The tragedy of women feeling that they never retire is that when they become widows, it's too late for them to discover the potential for joint retirement with their mate. What could have been life's best chapter for them with their mates never can be now because the mate is dead.

So retirement by widowhood is not a happy choice for most women. The death and absence of a departed husband often causes the widow's heart to grow fonder. But there is no need to idealize the past or refrain from being realistic about women and their own retirement roles in the present and future tense.

PREPARE FOR WIDOWHOOD RETIREMENT

It's a fact that almost half the wives in the United States become widows by age sixty-five, and the percentage of women who are widows increases progressively in each older age group (according to the U.S. Bureau of Census). There are well over ten million widows in the United States and over 175,000 new widows each year. Of course, many husbands become widowers also, but the percentage is only about one-fourth as great as that for women sixty-five and older. The reason for this fact is simply that wives live an average of seven to eight years longer than their husbands.

So wives need to prepare for the unchosen retirement of widowhood, and husbands need to help them. A good friend of mine worked part-time for the IRS during tax season to help callers know how to prepare their tax returns. For him it was a ministry, and he offered kind, gentle help to everyone he could.

In his work, he often had occasion to hear widows regretfully say, "If my husband were only alive, he would know what to do"—and other statements similar to that one. My friend knew I was writing this book, because I asked for his input. He told me to counsel husbands and wives to make plain and specific all the understandings and agreements they had had up to that point in their lives.

He meant that both mates should know their financial condition and all other legal matters the surviving mate would face at widowhood. We'll talk some more about this matter in a later chapter.

Without being morbid, it's realistic for most married women to face the fact they will likely experience the grief and sad retirement of widowhood. However, with good financial and legal knowledge and preparation, widows will not have to experience other avoidable griefs. The widow should be prepared to deal with her financial condition, income matters, tax matters, property ownership, wills and trusts, and so forth.

Women who have been homemakers need to know even before their husband's retirement that they themselves are entitled to Social Security benefits even if they haven't worked outside the home. Phyllis and I learned that fact after I retired, but she draws approximately half of the Social Security amount I do, and she seldom worked outside the home.

My own counsel is for mates to fully enjoy retirement together but for both of them to be prepared for the eventuality of widowhood. This counsel is realistic and wise. But upon a husband's retirement—and well before wives retire into widowhood and become singles—there is a valuable lesson for both husbands and wives to learn. It's possible, practicable, and ideal for husbands and wives to be alive and retired together. Couples need to become aware of and discover enriched retirement possibilities for both of them.

First, let's agree that retirement doesn't mean doing nothing, and it doesn't mean having no responsibilities. Even widows have things to do and some basic responsibilities as long as they are still able to function. I'm edging into the fact that retired husbands can and should take on part of whatever it is that keeps women from feeling they never retire. And most wives at retiree age and stage would do well to join a friend of mine in considering how far she had come from work-intensive years to her present state: namely, to semiretirement.

SEMIRETIREMENT

A friend of ours named Oakley Williams got offered an early retirement package. He decided to take the offer. His wife, Charline, was as excited as her husband about it. When I called their home, Charline was the first to share the good news with me, and I gave my congratulations. She told how she had also shared the good news at her beauty salon, where she was good friends with all the people. Then she confided to me that she was both puzzled and dismayed at her beauty salon friends' response to the news. They had unanimously bemoaned the husband's retirement by chorusing, "Oh, Charline, what are you going to do?"

Since I myself was a seasoned retiree at the time, I knew a bit about why Charline's friends were so concerned about what her husband's retirement might mean for her. But—ever the optimist—I told Charline that Oakley's retirement was a good thing for both of them and that they would have a great retirement together. I knew what I told Charline was true because she and Oakley had already had a great time together in the earlier chapters of their marriage.

Further, I told Charline that it was to be her retirement, too.

She replied perkily, "Oh, I've been semiretired for the last two or three years." She already knew the secret of a wife's retirement and had an insight about shared retirement with her husband. She had seen Oakley strained in the vast responsibilities of corporate life, the hassle of many miles of daily commuting, and long hours of work. She appreciated her husband's career, but she longed for him to get a new kind of life on a different plane and share it with her. And they've done that!

But back to semiretirement: What does that mean for women? Well, obviously, different things for different women. But within the context I'm focusing on right now, semiretirement is a call to compare and contrast early and middle married life with present and future married life.

For women married and with children, it is literally true that their work is never done. Even if the wife and mother has worked outside the home during all her children's growing-up years, it would be futile to try to list all the other work she has felt responsible for and has done. Typically, she has been all things to all family members and tried to meet their needs and wants. She has been mate, parent, lover, friend, counselor, cook, washerwoman, house-cleaner, emergency-service-worker, chauffeur, and anything else you care to add to the list.

As a rule, when the children get older and leave home, the wife is no longer responsible for all those things she had to do in earlier chapters of life. I'm aware that homes increasingly have (1) hanger-on children who don't leave, (2) other children who return home with their own children and refeather the empty nest, and (3) the possibility of caring for grandchildren. Nevertheless, wives normally graduate to a new plane of existence and a better work status as they grow older.

All you've just read may furrow your brow simply because

it isn't true in your case. Even if all the kids are gone from home, wives may not sense much lessening of demands on them personally by their husbands and others. But let me put a little flesh-and-blood history on semiretirement by referring to my own personal experience—without claiming that I have arrived as an ideal retired husband.

As I mentioned earlier, I was barely nineteen and Phyllis was seventeen when we got married. Marriage at any age is a risk, but young marriages often don't last. It's hard to discourage young people, so we went ahead and got married almost fifty years ago. Although we're still not sure it's going to work out, we're still happily married and happily retired.

As you would know, all the chapters of our marriage haven't been easy ones. For a number of years, we struggled financially for the necessities of life and a minimum comfort level. I was in college and graduate school for the first eight years, and Phyllis also went to school with me for two of those years. I was a full-time student, full-time secular worker, and part-time pastor most of those years.

Just after our first anniversary, we welcomed Mark as our firstborn. Before I finally got out of college and graduate school, we had two more sons. Phyllis had to learn to be a wife, a mother, and sometimes work outside the home, too. But mostly she was covered up with work at home. I kept telling her things would get better. When they didn't and I said that, she began to add, "In heaven."

Well, in time, things did get better, and neither one of us was yet in heaven. With God's provision and our hard work, financial burdens eased considerably through the middle years of our married lives. We began to enjoy sharing vacations and some leisure time. We raised our three boys with the goal of helping them become independent, and they grew to the point that they could take care of most of their own needs. So Phyllis began to experience a different level of work but still lots of work.

When the boys got out of school and got married, we were home alone. And things got even better in some ways. Every time one of the healthy, hungry boys left home, we felt like we got a pay raise because the food bill was so much lower. Our boys had worked and bought a lot of their clothes, but when they got out on their own, we no longer had to buy any of their clothes.

Sam Peter was our only dog, and he died at age fourteen. After that, we didn't even own goldfish. So even before retirement, with our nest empty of children and pets, we often took vacation and work trips together. We belatedly began to experience honeymoon times and locations that many married couples enjoy at the beginning of marriage. Grandchildren came along— four boys and four girls—and that was enriching, too. Things had gotten better.

We're old enough and had little enough money during the early years that Phyllis used a washboard to wash diapers on in early marriage. But those days were past, and through the middle years, we had a washer and dryer and most other conveniences of modern technology.

Not too many years before retirement, I bought a microwave. With the boys gone and just the two of us at home, Phyllis began to use the microwave regularly; most of the time big meals were appropriately a thing of the past. We began to eat out more often, and that took some burden off the cooking and dishwashing. I think you might get the right perspective if you compared and contrasted Phyllis's early washboard years with the later years I've just described. She certainly wasn't retired and still had husband Johnnie, but you might say she was semiretired.

For as long as I can remember, Phyllis has done lots of volunteer work and stayed productively busy. Those activities always were optional and continue to be optional. But as time went on and life's chapters unfolded, Phyllis began to have more leisure time to choose to work, play, pursue a hobby, take up something new, or to spend more time with me as we jointly made those choices.

Back to Charline Williams. Her married career of wife and mother was a good bit like Phyllis's married life—plus some work outside the home. So I understood what Charline meant when she said she had been pretty much semiretired for the last two or three years. She refused to indulge in a self-pity party and complain that women never retire. However, even semi-retirement is not the shared, full retirement possible for loving, compatible mates.

FULL RETIREMENT

How can a woman ever fully retire? Again, the answer to that question depends largely upon what full retirement is. Every year millions of women themselves retire from working outside the home, so they retire from full-time, paid employment. But any woman who is married or responsible for a household under-stands the nature of the question that asks whether a woman can ever fully retire. The heart of the question is this: Can a woman retire in leisure like her husband retires and not have to have an agenda? That's pretty much the question.

The answer to the question is no—unless a woman has a good understanding of what full retirement is. Further, the answer is still no unless she and her husband reach a happy agreement on a fully shared retirement. But with these caveats considered, the answer can be yes: A woman can fully retire with her mate—and not just retire alone when and if widowhood comes.

Retirement caveats for women. A caveat is a qualifier. The first qualifier I gave was that a woman has to have a good understanding of what full retirement is. So I would ask a woman to define what full retirement for her would mean. What would it include? What would it exclude? What would it take for a woman to say she is fully retired?

I haven't taken a survey on the matter, but I would be willing to guess that we might summarize full retirement for a woman. The wife wouldn't have to do anything that the husband didn't have to do. She wouldn't be expected to do anything for him that he wouldn't do for her. She would be able to do whatever she wanted to do, whenever she wanted to do it, and not have to answer to a boss or a husband. Would that be full retirement for a woman?

To be more specific and get house-oriented, the wife would not have to continue housework: no cooking, no washing of dishes or clothes, no making of beds, no vacuuming or dusting, no carrying out of the trash, no mowing and trimming of grass, no grocery shopping, and no house maintenance. That doesn't cover everything, but it's a pretty good list. Full retirement?

Full retirement misconceptions. Full retirement does not mean a holiday every day with no responsibilities and only complete rest or leisure. Retirement may appear to be all of that if the male mate is mean enough to take a sabbatical that doesn't equally include his wife. Retirement may appear that way if the husband selfishly models a self-indulgent retirement. But that is not the kind of retirement you've read about in this book for either mate. Husbands and wives have a mutual responsibility to each other as long as they both live and are able to be up and about. And there's a responsibility even in retirement beyond what each mate owes to the other. But, for now, let's take another tack on understanding full retirement for wives.

Expecting too much. If a woman thinks full retirement is retirement from all responsibilities, that's expecting too much and expecting the wrong thing. Neither the husband nor the wife is free to retire from all responsibilities or from reciprocal responsibilities to each other. But the reciprocal responsibilities necessarily and ideally change in retirement.

I honestly doubt that any husband and wife will ever get to the point of 100 percent equality in full retirement. But I do believe there can be a *fully shared retirement* that both husband and wife can enter into as the retirement transition occurs. For this to occur, it requires a joint effort just as getting married did.

FULLY SHARED RETIREMENT

It's not only appropriate for the wife to expect fully shared retirement, but it's something she should say out loud. I would envision the wife saying with joy to her husband at his retirement, "I want us both to enjoy a fully shared retirement." If that statement doesn't open the door to discuss the meaning of retirement for both husband and wife, it will at least plant the seed for cultivation. And when the thought is ripe, a couple will do well to envision the happiness potential for both of them in this era of life.

Before retirement, the traditional role called for the husband to bring home the bacon and for the wife to cook it. Let that thought stand for all the different things husbands and wives have done in preretirement as a general division of labor. With good financial planning and good fortune, the husband's days of bringing home the bacon may be mostly over, but the wife may feel she still has to cook the bacon. In other words, if the husband retires from work to play and the wife continues to have the same level of work, she doesn't have a retirement—certainly not a retirement equal to the husband's. Something about that scenario needs to change.

Full retirement for the wife ideally calls for her to share the retirement party with her husband. It's her retirement, too. Without abruptness or abrasiveness, a gradual and mutual agreement on a new division of labor at home needs to occur.

Full retirement for women exists only if it is a fully shared retirement between husband and wife. What the husband was excused from doing all the years he was laboring outside the home, he is no longer excused from. It is not a marriage of mutual love and respect for the wife to continue to do everything she has done all through the marriage years and for the husband to watch her while he does nothing. Even if the wife might be considered semiretired compared to early and middle marriage, the retirement is still not rightly shared if the husband does not assume a fair share of the labor the couple is jointly responsible for.

Men Helping Women Retire

I suppose Simone de Beauvoir was right when she wrote, "The most sympathetic of men never fully comprehend woman's concrete situation" (*The Second Sex*). But personally, I believe that a lot of men come to realize their own retirement is incomplete as long as their wives, their other selves, remain at work. As Elizabeth Cady Stanton said, "So long as women are slaves, men will be knaves."

Let me share a little personal history at this point. When I retired, I hadn't even been mowing the grass. After the boys grew up and left home, Phyllis took over that job. I traveled away from home about 120 workdays a year and was stretched from morning to night in corporate work. Phyllis did pretty much everything at home, and her responsibilities fell under the umbrella of what chauvinists or jokesters refer to as "woman's work."

Genderless work. After I was retired for a while, it gradually occurred to me that I wasn't doing man's work or woman's work. I was just loafing, and Phyllis was doing all the work. Being mostly a decent sort of guy, I began to quit using a gender to describe any kind of work. Work was work that needed to be done whether a woman did it or a man did it. My concern about a macho image went down the drain, and I wasn't afraid of looking like a hen-pecked husband.

The grass needed mowing, and I knew how to mow grass; so I took over that job. When Phyllis sealed up a bag full of trash, I began to think I probably ought to take it outside to the trash container—and maybe even start gathering it and putting it in the bag. Gradually, I noticed that the bed was still unmade while Phyllis was fixing breakfast. It dawned on me that the least I could do was make up the bed each day, so I took over that little job, and eventually a few other jobs.

Learning how to vacuum. Though there are exceptions, it's generally true that men are not skilled in housework. Men don't know where dust resides. Their culinary skills are confined to digital cooking: That means dialing for pizza to be delivered or punching numbers on the microwave. But in retirement, men who want to can and should learn some homemaking skills.

For example, as Phyllis continued her busy volunteer work outside the home—and I did my own retirement stuff—I began to think that perhaps I could learn to vacuum the floor. While Phyllis was gone, I began to experiment at vacuuming. Right up front, I found that I didn't like the vacuum cleaner we had; it wasn't powerful enough. So I did Internet research and bought a new and better vacuum cleaner. (I've bought five of them since I retired.) Then I began to learn how to vacuum and to do an excellent job of it. An old dog may not be able to learn new tricks, but a willing husband can.

Well, Phyllis nearly fell over when I took the initiative to vacuum. She thanked me profusely and told me what a good job I did. Now, men, this is not the time to beam over your new skill or to make a big deal out of beginning to do what your wife has done for umpteen years. Rather, it's time to pooh-pooh what you've done as being very little and to express gratitude to your wife for having done that chore through all your marriage years. Without wanting men to have an ulterior motive, I just want them to know that learning to vacuum the floors may be the greatest aphrodisiac they'll discover on Planet Earth.

Discovering aptitude. After the first sabbatical of retirement is over, it's a good idea to let a husband discover some of the things he might want to do around the house. It doesn't hurt to plant the seed and cultivate it, but the husband needs to develop a want-to. If the guy is a bum and always has been, he'll likely remain one. But if both husband and wife buy into the concept of a woman sharing fully in retirement, then the door is open for a new division of labor and a reciprocal approach to joint responsibilities.

THE JOY OF JOINT RETIREMENT

Since I have much more leisure time in retirement, I've tried to take part of the homework off Phyllis so she, too, can have more leisure time—more optional time. Without splitting up percentages in a contrived division of labor, we've moved forward happily to help each other.

Now, I know I haven't arrived at Saint Husbandhood and probably never will. But the point is that I've begun to assume a shared responsibility for the household. Some of the things Phyllis once had to do if they were to get done, she no longer has to do. So she's retired from those activities. And although her retirement is not equal to mine, she's made headway, and so have I. These steps toward joint retirement have brought Phyllis and me mutual joy.

I will never be superior to Phyllis, but I have tried to set her free. The freedom is not the kind that has separated us in any way; rather, it's the kind that has drawn us together even more. Husbands have the potential to try to free their wives in a similar way—regardless of their specific retirement circumstances.

WHEN WOMEN AND MEN RETIRE

Besides all the work Phyllis does at home, she continues to teach English as a second language, lead a nursing home ministry she started over thirty years ago, and write professionally. Besides the shared work I do at home, I also continue to write and do other kinds of work for pay. But I find jobs in which I'm freely helping others without charge or financial compensation to be special. So both Phyllis and I continue to work in all the ways we want to.

Some people look at both of us and tell us we're not really retired. When we hear someone say that, we feel complimented, because we understand retirement as the dessert chapter of life that builds on all the other chapters. But in receiving that compliment, we also hear some implication that the one bestowing it thinks of retirement as full leisure without work and commitments. Now, Phyllis and I know that we really are retired. But obviously, retirement doesn't mean to us what it means to a lot of other folks.

It's worth repeating: Retirement is optional time to choose what, when, where, and how we work or play. The retirement accent is on leisure time and how best to use it. We choose to make commitments and be productive in part of our optional time, and we choose to rest or play or travel in the other part of our leisure time. So we are retired—or at least semiretired. And as we move on through the minichapters of retirement, we're enjoying giving it our best shot at mutual retirement and with a sense of stewardship for our lives.

Yes, women can retire—before widowhood. And men can help them retire. In fact, this mutual retirement is the only way for "one flesh" to experience full retirement.

REFLECTIONS AND PROJECTIONS

- What was your thinking about women and retirement before you read this chapter? Any changes in your thinking? If so, what?
- Looking back, what would have been your ideal marriage division of labor?
- Identify what you consider an ideal retirement division of labor for mates.
- Complete this sentence: Women retire when. . . .

RETIREMENT WORDS FROM THE WORD

Proverbs 31:31; Ephesians 4:32; Ephesians 5:22; Ephesians 5:32; Ecclesiastes 3:1; Ecclesiastes 3:12–13

PRAYER THOUGHTS

Father, help me to be more concerned about Your will for my life than about my gender. Help me to remember that I, too, was created in Your image and was created for rest as well as for work. Match me with my mate in retirement, and help us to love and respect each other in this special season of life. Amen.

CHAPTER SEVEN

BODY AND. . .

*The human body is an instrument
for the production of the human soul.*

ALFRED NORTH WHITEHEAD

T his chapter and the next deal with having the right body-and-soul perspective in retirement. The focus is largely on not letting your body and soul go to pot during your retirement years. Although retirement normally includes living with a mate, a family, friends, or some kind of group, there are body-and-soul choices that no one but you can make in retirement. So it's important to have the right commitment and make the right choices about both body and soul.

A MATTER OF PERSPECTIVE

If a person holds a distorted view of retirement, he may consider himself old overnight and let his mind tell him what he can't do anymore. Philosopher Elton Trueblood used to counsel, "Don't retire from everything at once; rather, retire from one thing at a time, gradually and as you want to or have to." This counsel is especially important in dealing with the physical and the spiritual aspects of retirement.

Premature aging can come from disease, stress, the genes, inactivity, or from a faulty retirement mind-set. Inactivity and a faulty retirement mind-set are factors a retiree specifically can choose to avoid. We all have to get older, but we don't have to get old or give up on productive living.

When Is Old?

Jimmy Carter answered this question by saying that old is when we think we are (*The Virtues of Aging*). Baseball great Satchel Paige asked, "How old would you be if you didn't know how old you was?" Bernard Baruch said, "Old age is always fifteen years older than I am" (*The Ultimate Book of Business Quotations*). When humorist James Thurber entered his sixties, he said, "If there were fifteen months in every year, I'd only be forty-eight. That's the trouble with us. We number everything."

Carter, Thurber, and Paige were saying that age is largely a matter of perspective. The birth certificate and calendar tell us how many years old we are chronologically, but they don't tell us how much life we've got in us or how many more years we'll live. We know some cars don't last one hundred thousand miles while others last as many as five hundred thousand miles. Every now and then I still see someone on the road in a Model T Ford. Now, I admit that a Model T Ford is old, but the ones I see on the road are still running and have life left in them.

How much life a person has within him is reflected more by

the soul than by the body. The body may show all kinds of wear and tear while the inner being might be better tuned than it was at the beginning. Without making light of the heaviness of an aging body, there is a retirement lesson for us here.

DON'T LET RETIREMENT CRIPPLE YOU

I used to enjoy reading the cartoon strip *Andy Capp* before our paper quit including it. The cartoon strip was mostly satire about Andy as an unemployed, worthless skunk of a husband contrasted with the virtues of his hardworking wife, Flo. On one occasion when Flo was worn to a nub and Andy was going out to play soccer, she commented, "You always said we would grow old together." Andy replied, "Yes, but you went off and left me, didn't you?"

Husbands and wives can help each other keep from getting an old-age mind-set. One lighthearted example from our home came when Phyllis began to have difficulty reading the letters of newspaper-sized type right in front of her. She thought she was going blind and went to see Dr. Burkett Nelson, our family optometrist.

When Phyllis got home from her eye checkup, she announced somewhat gravely to me that she had *presbyopia*. She wanted my sympathy; but since I had majored in Greek, I already knew that *presbyopia* just meant "elder eyes." After about age forty, most folks begin to experience some presbyopia, which shows up in decreased elasticity of the lens and focusing problems on small print. Bifocals take care of the problem. Phyllis's eyes had gotten older, but she was just as young at heart and mischievous as ever. She'll never get an old-age mind-set.

An acquaintance of mine's husband had heart surgery a second time. When the doctor came out of the operating room, he told the apprehensive wife that her husband had come through the surgery well. Fearful that he might be a cardiac cripple, she anxiously asked, "Will he have a good quality of life?"

The surgeon replied, "I don't know. I fixed his heart; the quality of life is up to him." And the last time I checked, he was still choosing to have a great quality of life.

A HEALTHY RECKLESSNESS

Get an annual physical. Many people have gotten annual work physicals and need to keep that up even if they no longer work for a company that will pay for them. Others who have worked inside or outside the home may not have gotten annual physicals. But retirees need one at least once a year. Persius, a Roman satirist, said, "Meet the disease at its first stage." Proverbial truth wisely counsels that a stitch in time saves nine, and an ounce of prevention is worth a pound of cure. It's wise to get a physical each year, but it's also wise not to become anxious or obsessed about what may or may not be wrong with the body.

Don't be a hypochondriac. The only thing some people seem to have on their minds is what's wrong with them. They're hypochondriacs. Basically, hypochondria is to be depressed or obsessive about health problems whether they're real or imagined. A cure I once read for hypochondriacs is to have a healthy recklessness about their physical condition. The point of the counsel was that people can make their minds sick by worrying about their body.

When the doctor diagnoses a condition, it's usually a good

idea to accept that diagnosis and also the treatment prescribed for the condition. Or get a second medical opinion. But if a doctor can't find anything wrong with you, it's usually a good idea to avoid letting the mind find anything wrong.

Josh Billings said, "There's lots of people in this world who spend so much time watching their health that they haven't the time to enjoy it." Laurence Sterne wrote, "People who are always taking care of their health are like misers, who are hoarding up a treasure which they have never spirit enough to enjoy" (*The Doctor's Quotation Book*).

Those quotes reminded me of a funny incident that happened when I was in a senior health fair line a few years ago. One of my elderly friends in front of me had just gotten the results of his total blood cholesterol count. He complained, "I haven't had a sausage biscuit in six months, and my cholesterol isn't down a single point."

I said, "John, I believe I'd chance one."

My suggestion wasn't dietary advice but a plea for some balance between body and soul. William Butler Yeats wrote,

> *An aged man is but a paltry thing*
> *A tattered coat upon a stick, unless*
> *Soul clap its hands and sing, and louder sing*
> *For every tatter in its mortal dress.*

There's got to be a time to clap and sing or else what's the use of living? But it's still a good idea to carefully choose a doctor who can help you manage and balance your health as you go along life's way clapping and singing.

CHOOSING A RETIREMENT DOCTOR

Changing doctors? You may have a fine doctor you're able to continue with right on into your retirement. However, many people have to change doctors because they change locations when they retire. Others have to change doctors because of problems with insurance coverage. And some people have to choose another doctor because they either outlive their doctor or find the doctor joining them in retirement. Retirees especially need a doctor they trust, click with, and are willing to partner with in taking care of body and soul. Although no doctor will likely meet all your needs, it's a good idea to have in mind the qualities you want in the doctor you choose.

Choose one with a good memory. At a minimum, choose a doctor whose memory is better than yours. Choose one who takes good notes and reads your file each time before he meets with you. Some years ago I had a doctor who took me off blood-pressure medicine he had prescribed. Then at each of the next three meetings we had, he began by asking, "Are you still taking your blood-pressure medicine?" Each time, I tactfully reminded him that he had taken me off blood-pressure medicine but that I would be glad to start taking it again if he felt I needed it. The doctor would look puzzled and then move on. Now, do you want your life in the hands of a doctor like that? I didn't either, so I changed doctors.

Choose a practicing doctor. A doctor with top-notch medical skills is a priority for all of us, but there are other factors to consider, too. A doctor ought to practice what he preaches and what he expects you to follow. The ancient Greek medical expert Galen wrote, "That physician will hardly be thought very careful of the health of others who neglects his own."

Consider whether the doctor himself is fat, smokes, drinks, has a religious faith, is punctual or apologetic, knows how to talk heart-to-heart as well as face-to-face, and has a sense of humor. In good humor, one doctor was able to tell his obese patient, "Your body is a temple, but your congregation is too large."

In short, choose a doctor you like, can trust, and will obey. Choose a doctor who can detect whether you've come to him with a life-threatening runny nose or whether you are really sick.

Choose a human being. When I confessed to one doctor that I ate a cheeseburger, he didn't chide me but said, "Well, all of us are going to die of something, and it's good to get some enjoyment out of life." I liked that. But great concern for patient health causes some doctors to be very strict in what they prescribe. That fact led Sir Francis Bacon to write, "The remedy is worse than the disease."

G. K. Chesterton struck a blow for humanity when he wrote, "Man does not live by soap alone, and hygiene, or even health, is not much good unless you can take a healthy view of it—or, better still, feel a healthy indifference to it" (*All I Survey*, "On St. George Revivified"). So doctor and patient ideally have a happy partnership.

PARTNERING WITH YOUR DOCTOR

Prepare for your visits. Once you've chosen a doctor, partner with that doctor instead of letting him be the boss with you as the employee. For example, I prepare a single-sheet, typed summary to hand my doctor each time we meet. The sheet is dated, has the doctor's name, my name, all medications I'm taking, any changes since the last visit, and why I'm visiting this time. I keep a copy in my files and give the doctor one for his files. And I tell the doctor what I expect, hope, or need to know at this visit. Your doctor will appreciate this kind of partnering.

Be honest. You'll get your best help if you're honest with your doctor. The doctor needs to know all the prescribed medications, unprescribed medications, vitamins, herbs, and other things you take. The doctor can't help you if you beat around the bush about sexual dysfunction, male or female problems, or symptoms you would rather ignore than reveal. So be honest, be candid, and identify your priority health concerns.

Don't overexpect. Although it's not too much to expect your doctor to believe in miracles, it is too much to expect the doctor to perform miracles. You and your doctor should have a pretty fair understanding of what you both expect. A woman in her eighties complained to her doctor about her aches and pains. He listened sympathetically and responded, "You must understand, my dear, I'm a doctor, not a magician. I cannot make you any younger."

"Younger?" she said. "No, I'm asking you to make me older, Doctor."

Be resilient. As you age, the doctor's report will not always be good; chances are that you'll have to learn to live with some chronic health problems. I once read that the way to live to a ripe old age is to get a chronic disease and nurture it. Besides, some of history's greatest works have come from people who were in the midst of chronic, acute, or terminal illnesses. They would not let their soul be defeated by their body, so they won with their spirit. Many people refuse to quit living just because they are dying. They're determined to live until they do die.

We do not choose our diseases or traumas, but we can choose to be a winner instead of just a survivor. We can choose to bounce back or even crawl back from trauma and adversity. We can endure, have hope, and live a quality life despite having a body that has seen its best days.

Have an agreement. When the doctor has done all he can, and your body and soul have done all they can, what's next? Living wills can spell out that next step, but the living person and the attending doctor already need to have a specific agreement of heart and mind. The choice is yours, but be aware that "body and mind, like man and wife, do not always agree to die together" (Charles Colton). I've seen what happens when a mind dies before the body. I've made my choice so that both family and physician know what I want done if my mind dies before my body. Specifically, they know I don't want any heroic efforts made to extend the life of a mindless body. My decision agrees with what Lord Thomas Horder said the year before I was born: "It is the duty of a doctor to prolong life. It is not his duty to prolong the act of dying." There is a time to live and a time to die.

THE BEST RX I EVER HAD

But to get back to the living part, it was just over forty years ago that Dr. Robert Bone gave me the best prescription I ever had. I was a seminary student who acted as if I were Superman and didn't have a breaking point. But I learned differently. Here's what led me to Dr. Bone: I had a full school load, commuted 225 miles roundtrip per day, supported a wife and three children, pastored a church full time, and slept little or stayed up all night to get everything done. Up to that time I didn't have a doctor because I didn't need one. Until I nearly collapsed.

Dr. Bone examined me and learned that I was wondering how a person of faith could cave in physically. Then he said, "Johnnie, you don't have a faith problem; you have a physical problem." He explained I was suffering from exhaustion, being overweight, and not getting any exercise.

When Dr. Bone mentioned golf as a possible exercise, I told him I didn't have time or money to play golf. So he gave me this prescription: "When you leave this office, drive straight to the nearest sporting-goods store and buy a good jump rope. Then jump that rope every day." Despite the fact I was almost broke, I did what Dr. Bone said and bought a three-dollar jump rope. Then I began to jump the rope every day until I built up to one thousand jumps a day. And I began to get in shape and get well.

In the forty-plus years since then, I've religiously continued the jump rope prescription. I've jumped rope and shaken homes and hotel rooms all over the United States and in numerous foreign countries. Even today when colleagues and friends from the past see me, one of the first questions they usually ask is, "Johnnie, are you still jumping your rope?" And I'm glad to answer yes.

Second son Larry said over thirty years ago, "Dad, one of these days you're going to get too old to jump that rope."

I replied, "Yep, but until then, I'm going to keep on jumping." Then after about thirty years had passed, Larry wrote a Father's Day article about me for a local newspaper and said, "Not even jump rope manufacturers can predict the performance of a new type of jump rope the way he can."

And I'm still at it today—after wearing out a bunch of jump ropes. But now I alternate days of jumping rope and walking three miles with Phyllis. Interestingly, I visited Dr. Bone not long ago, and our picture was taken with me holding the original but worn-out jump rope he had prescribed in 1963. And I told him it was the best and cheapest prescription I ever had.

Now in the twenty-first century, jumping rope is a team sport and is widely popular. But what are the benefits of jumping a rope? For me, I lost weight, got aerobically fit, improved hand-eye coordination, and jumping rope seemed to help my racquetball game. Jumping rope got me started on a systematic exercise program. The program is portable, inexpensive, and doesn't depend on the weather.

However, I need to caution you that jumping rope is not for everyone. Through the years, my testimony about this best prescription has motivated a lot of other people to start jumping rope. Some of them have reported back to me about pulled muscles, sore knees, splinters, and other injuries. So I don't recommend rope jumping for everyone.

In my first year of retirement, I read that older people often keep up their aerobic capacity but lose a lot of their upper body strength. So I began to lift pairs of five-, ten-, and fifteen-pound weights each morning to tone and maintain upper body strength. Besides jumping rope and lifting weights, my exercise program includes a variety of floor exercises, playing racquetball, cutting and splitting firewood, hiking, and walking with Phyllis.

Now, what I do is nothing to brag about, and the results aren't all that great to look at. But what I do is a stewardship effort to maintain and develop the potential of my God-given body. For a productive retirement, I counsel you to work with a doctor first to find out what your physical condition is and what kind of exercise prescription he recommends for you. And if you don't have an exercise program, you need a conversion to one that you will follow religiously.

EXERCISE THE BODY

Retirement transitions. I've read that retirees gain about one pound per year. Retirement tends to change activity patterns and eating patterns. Usually, the person who had to get up every morning no longer has to. You may no longer have a routine that expends calories in preparing for work, going to work, actually working, and possibly exercising at some health facility during the day. The refrigerator is just a few steps away now instead of miles away, and your stash of junk food may even be closer. I've observed that people tend to gain weight when they retire unless they consciously and consistently work at maintaining an optimum weight—or at least work to avoid gaining weight.

Stewards of the body. Some people love to say that when they think of exercise they lie down until the thought passes. Others humorously say that they get their exercise being pallbearers at the funerals of their friends who exercised. But those who have studied the matter know that exercise can be a powerful factor in both quality of life and length of life. Although the apostle Paul didn't put physical exercise on a par with spiritual exercise, he did recognize its value (1 Timothy 4:8 NIV). Besides all that, we're accountable for the use or disuse of our bodies. The Bible tells us that our bodies are temples of the Holy Spirit (1 Corinthians 6:19–20).

Philosopher Herbert Spencer wrote, "The preservation of health is a duty." In fact, taking care of the body is a sacred duty that calls for self-discipline. Dramatist Henrik Ibsen had an opinion about those who neglect this duty: "People who don't know how to keep themselves healthy ought to have the decency to get themselves buried, and not waste time about it" (*When We Dead Awaken*). My feelings about the matter aren't that abrasive, but I do strongly believe each of us is responsible for learning how to take care of body and soul and for making a commitment to have the self-discipline to do it.

Keeping the body fit. Over thirty years ago, Phyllis began to be bothered with poor circulation and a chronic condition of limbs going to sleep both during the day and during the night. I told her she needed to do some exercise. She responded by telling me she did housework, gardened, and other things that were exercise. But from my own experience, I realized that what she was doing wasn't getting the exercise job done satisfactorily to match her body's needs.

So once again I practiced medicine without a license and counseled her to at least try an aerobic exercise program for a while. She took my suggestion and started jogging. In just a month or two of jogging and walking, her circulation problems cleared up. Now, over a generation later, she walks three miles a day at a good pace and still has good circulation. She's also learned to split firewood.

Some people think they're too old to start exercising. They have adopted a crippling old-age mind-set instead of following the good example of other older citizens. My mother started exercising twice a day after she reached eighty and then got exercise training at a rehab center after a fall. She said a therapist taught her to exercise every muscle in her body and that it helped her arthritis and relieved other pains. Mother said on more than one occasion that she would become an invalid if she quit exercising. So she exercised morning and evening almost all of her octogenarian days until she died at eighty-nine.

Other models for me of exercising even into one's nineties have included Luck Henson and Oliver Dean. In his nineties, Luck was still walking around an indoor track most days. He was stooped, held a cane in one hand and the track rail in the other hand; he moved slowly but kept right on walking and exercising. Oliver Dean had passed his ninety-sixth birthday and was struggling with a walker when I last saw him playing pool with friends at a Christian activity center.

There are more striking examples of people exercising and competing in athletics in their seniors years, but I've just told you about some of those closest to me. Although there are scientific studies and statistics that prove the value of exercise, I've chosen to give you personal testimony and observations that exercise in retirement is of great value.

NOURISH THE BODY

A changing diet. As we move on in retirement, we may have to give up a lot of activities we once enjoyed, but we never retire from eating. I read that the body is an autobiography of a person's life. Whether that's true or not, I don't know. But the body does tend to reflect a lifetime of exercise and eating habits. And the diet most prescribed for retirees often calls for a radical change in food selections from what they've enjoyed in earlier years.

Mark Twain caused Pudd'nhead Wilson to say, "The only way to keep your health is to eat what you don't want, drink what you don't like, and do what you'd rather not." Giving up sugar, fat, salt, and cholesterol may take much of the flavor out of eating and the enjoyment out of what we like to taste. But I believe there's a sensible approach that balances a changing diet with a continuing appetite for what we like to eat.

Learn what's best. Doctors, dieticians, and wise laypersons can identify the kind of diet that best contributes to good health and longevity. Most of us share some ignorance about the kind of diet that is best for us. Oh, we may know we need to cut down on fat, reduce salt, and watch calories. But we may not be aware that canned soups contain a lot of sodium. We may not know the difference in saturated fats and unsaturated fats. The event of a heart attack or some other health crisis is a hard way to learn an easy lesson. A part of good stewardship of life is to learn what is best for us to eat and to make healthy eating our regular way of eating.

Appetites and aberrations. Normally we eat healthy at our house. That's mainly because Phyllis prepares broccoli, cauliflower, asparagus, and other vegetables that I would never choose at a cafeteria or bring home from a grocery store. I wonder along with the youngsters why you never hear about anything like mad cauliflower disease.

When Phyllis and I go to a cafeteria and I order a vegetable plate, she tells me that what I select is a starch plate. For many of us, what we like seems to be bad for us, and what we don't like is high on the list of being good for us. One youngster prayed, "Dear Lord, thank You for this healthy meal, and please help us to be able to eat it." I identify with that prayer.

I do like the basic vegetables that come on a hamburger. And Phyllis offers me lots of opportunities to eat fruits, which I enjoy. She serves a well-balanced and nourishing diet often graced with good seasonings and tasty sauces that disguise some foods. But Phyllis also has the wisdom to know a steady diet of healthy food doesn't satisfy some of our lifetime appetites and longings.

So on rare occasions we indulge in an aberration from our healthy diet. For example, one morning I was shaving while Phyllis was fixing breakfast. I sniffed the aroma of what I knew had to be a wonderful breakfast I could give thanks for without hypocrisy. Phyllis was cooking sausage, eggs mingled with onions and peppers, cheese grits, and homemade biscuits. Along with all that, I smelled the scent of strong coffee that was "leaded."

We ate like there would be no tomorrow. But the next day it was back to bagels, cereal, and the like because we do want to experience a lot of tomorrows.

Tasty, healthful foods. One of the benefits of modern technology is that we're beginning to have more and more foods that are both healthy and tasty. I've been wowed with fat-free potato chips. Decaffeinated coffee has reached a new plateau of taste. Some sandwiches and other foods have just a few fat grams and not too many calories. So it's possible to enjoy a healthy diet that keeps tabs on fat, calories, sodium, carbohydrates, and cholesterol content without being paranoid or obnoxious to others about the menu.

Eating and abstaining. It's been said that some people live to eat while others eat to live. In retirement, it's not enough to know what to eat and what not to eat. We need to know when to eat and when not to eat. Nourishing the body calls for eating regular meals, but it also calls for abstaining from recreational eating that may amount to all-day grazing.

One extreme we sometimes see in retirement is the loss of appetite and a carelessness about eating enough to nourish the body. But the more frequent occurrence is for retirees to eat recreationally as a pastime, filling the body with calories when we're not even hungry. Also, retirement tends to tempt us with too many social opportunities to eat more than we should. Many of us gain weight when we need to be losing weight.

Most of our adult lives, Phyllis and I have weighed ourselves every day. Then I've recorded our weights in a daily diary. The number of pounds we weigh usually affects the choice and quantity of what we eat each day. Although we could both stand to lose a few pounds, we have an overall commitment to keep from ballooning up in weight. My personal goal and my counsel for others is to nourish the body by eating wisely.

THE SOUL CONNECTION

An itinerant evangelist of another era worked himself to death. As he lay dying, he was heard to say that he had "killed the horse, which must carry the mail." My uncle Charlie Aiken put it another way. As he approached eighty, he had to deal with surgeries that came in staccato sequence, and he said, "I was busy keeping my mind in order, and my body fell apart."

The two quotes you've just read summarize what I've tried to say in this chapter on body. To go back to the beginning of the chapter, Alfred North Whitehead said, "The human body is an instrument for the production of the human soul." Let's be sure to make the body-soul connection.

The body is not more important than the soul, but it is part of our total being and is essential to complete our calling on earth. In retirement, most of us can improve or maintain our health. But even if health deteriorates, medical science and technology provide numerous ways to compensate for losses or deficiencies. We owe it to our souls to take good care of our bodies and to use them well.

REFLECTIONS AND PROJECTIONS

- Consider to what extent this statement applies to you: "If I had known I was going to live this long, I would have taken better care of my body."
- What personal choices have most hurt your body? Helped your body?
- Complete this sentence: As I grow older, I will stay young by...
- Write on a calendar the date by which you will have completed this year's physical (including mammogram or prostate check) and teeth and eye checkups.
- Choose one exercise your doctor approves for you to do daily (for example, walk a mile or stretch your limbs for a few minutes).
- Weigh yourself today, write it down, and commit that you will not gain a pound this year. (If you need to gain weight, commit to gaining an appropriate amount.)

RETIREMENT WORDS FROM THE WORD

Daniel 1:12, 15; Luke 12:22–23; 1 Peter 5:7; 1 Corinthians 6:19–20

PRAYER THOUGHTS

Father, thank You for the gift of my body and all that nourishes and sustains it. May I not give up on my earthly body before I finish doing what You have called me to do with it. Help me renew my commitment to be a good steward of my body and to turn all of my anxieties about it over to You. Amen.

Chapter Eight

. . .Soul

All great art is the work of the whole living creature,
body and soul, and chiefly of the soul.

John Ruskin

Actually, body and soul go together, so this chapter is a continuation of the preceding chapter. However, the focus on soul ascends to a higher level of personhood than what you've just read about the body that wears out and dies. The soul is created within time and eternity but doesn't end for all eternity. Though the soul may grow weary, it need not deteriorate or become less than what it has been. In fact, Hippocrates said, "The human soul develops up to the time of death."

And I would add that there is no evidence that the human soul quits developing even at death. Rather, I agree with Goethe, who wrote, "I am fully convinced that the soul is indestructible, and that its activity will continue through eternity. It is like the sun, which, to our eyes, seems to set in night; but it has in reality only gone to diffuse its light elsewhere."

GETTING A HANDLE ON SOUL

It's hard to get a handle on what *soul* means because there are so many different viewpoints about it. Without my claiming to be a philosopher or a theologian, it's important for you to know where I'm coming from as I speak of soul. Otherwise, we might not be reading from the same page, so to speak.

For me, soul refers to all that's involved in ongoing personhood: the total being. When I speak of soul, here's what I mean: the heart, mind, spirit, intellect, will, emotions, vitality, and person clothed in a recognizable body—both in this life and beyond. Body and soul make up the whole person. Even when the earthly body and soul are separated by death, God has provided for continuing recognition of persons in a resurrection body fit for all eternity (2 Corinthians 4:14–5:10). Theologian Christian Wolf wrote, "A person is not at any time viewed as a bodyless soul" (*Holman Bible Dictionary*, "Soul").

Claude Hailey is a friend of mine who owns a 1965 Chevelle. In his home garage, I was able to recognize the model without Claude having to identify it for me. However, the 1965 Chevrolet is far better than it was when the car was brand-new and came off the assembly line.

Over twenty years ago, Claude found the worn-out car sitting in a field on blocks with a two-hundred-dollar FOR SALE sign on it. He bought the old car. After that, Claude sandblasted and rebuilt the car from the ground up with premium parts, put chrome on the engine, and put a polished finish on the body. Claude still works on improving that car in one way or another on a regular basis. And that Chevelle has won numerous trophies in car shows.

Claude's car is better than it ever was before he got hold of it—better than when it came off the assembly line. I like to think that's just a pale comparison of the difference between our body on earth and the resurrection body God has for us. And I can't imagine God doing less for our minds than He plans to do for our bodies. We're fearfully and wonderfully made, but we're going to get even better in the resurrection.

Just as we have looked at the body in retirement, now let's look at the soul in retirement. Chances are that on earth the retirement soul may be in worse shape than the retirement body.

Getting Body and Soul Together

I am so busy. Wayne Muller wrote that across all of society's mosaic he hears the same refrain: "I am so busy" (*Remembering the Sacred Rhythm of Rest and Delight*). I've heard stressed-out people complain they're so busy that their soul needs to catch up with their body. And if we're not careful, this busyness may carry over into retirement.

Don't overschedule. A retirement cliché says, "I'm so busy that I don't know when I had time to work." If a retiree says he's too busy, something's wrong; for by definition retirement means choosing what to do with leisure time. There is a fine balance between choosing to do too much and choosing to do too little. We become more like ourselves as we get older. We don't mask our feelings as much, and it's okay to honestly say, "I don't think I want to do that." Retirement truly is a time to get body and soul together. It's a time to retire from "the madding crowd" so that we won't live life's last chapter in a hurry or a frenzy.

I think of Jesus who retired from time to time for prayer and solitude and then came back to minister to the madding crowd. But He Himself never seemed to hurry even when others wanted to hurry Him. He gave us a lesson for all of life but one we especially need to learn and live in retirement.

Start sooner. By nature, my dad disliked hurrying. He was a truck driver who orchestrated the gears on a semi and paced himself through lights and traffic. However, he worked a lifetime of meeting schedules others set for him. Then when Dad retired and anyone tried to hurry him, he would say, "If I had known I was going to have to hurry, I would have started sooner." Dad chose the right body-and-soul priority.

Novelist Kazuo Ishiguro said, "It is one of the enjoyments of retirement that you are able to drift through the day at your own pace" (*The Ultimate Book of Business Quotations*). Historian Will Durant observed, "No man who is in a hurry is quite civilized" (*Reader's Digest*, April 1999). Whether we drift or drive at our own pace, it's important not to feel driven and to be civilized rather than part of a rat race. There may be a time to hurry, but it's not all the time.

Choose what you want to maintain. A hippie once said to a rich man, "A lot of stuff sure does own you, doesn't it?" Etty Hillesum wrote in her diary, "Now that I don't want to own anything anymore and am free, now I suddenly own everything, now my inner riches are immeasurable." If our possessions burden us more than they lift us, then they own us instead of our owning them.

Retirement is a good time to downsize possessions and things that require a lot of maintenance. Every possession requires maintenance even if it's no more than a place to put it. The booming storage rental business is one evidence our society is owned by too much stuff. Folks don't know where to put it; so they rent space outside their homes. This kind of downsizing at retirement illustrates that less may be more in quality of life.

Retirees may need to downsize their housing, yard, garden, equipment, and total responsibilities.

But after doing a full inventory, a retiree may decide he doesn't want to downsize anything. If so, there's a lot to be said for outsourcing—paying someone else to do—what requires so much time that the soul feels harried and hurried.

NECESSITIES OF THE SOUL

Henry David Thoreau wrote, "Money is not required to buy one necessity of the soul." His thought set me to identifying the necessities of the soul. I don't know what those necessities are for others, but I do know what they are for me.

I came face-to-face with the necessities of the soul once when I was traveling and an anxious flight attendant told us we needed to prepare for a crash landing. The pilot said a tire had blown on takeoff from Nashville, and indicators were that our landing gear might not have "integrity." Well, the plane later landed safely, but during the crisis, I felt the need to identify my soul priorities and be at peace as we circled the Pittsburgh airport to use up explosive fuel.

My decision to receive Christ and be born again stood head and shoulders over all other soul necessities. That decision was essential for time and eternity beyond time. Besides the priority of being born again, other necessities for the health and welfare of my soul came to mind. Some of the soul necessities I identified could be helpful to others. So I'll share more and give some counsel.

Be born again. I've enjoyed friendship and eternal life with God ever since I made a personal commitment to accept Jesus

Christ as my Lord and Savior at age seven. Religious faith in God is a personal choice, but I believe it is essential for the soul to have eternal life instead of eternal death.

It is possible to retire—and to die—without ever having met this necessity of the soul. God loved us and gave His only Son to provide for our soul's necessity. God's gift truly is free to those who will receive it (John 3; Ephesians 2:8–10). If you've reached retirement age without personally trusting God in Christ, it's time for you to take care of the supreme soul necessity and be born again.

One fresh morning in the mountains, a friend of mine breathed in deep and exclaimed to a service station attendant, "Isn't it great to be alive!"

The attendant replied, "I don't know; I ain't never been any other way." Wrong. Everyone is dead in his sins and trespasses until he lets Christ make him alive through God's grace (Ephesians 2:1–6). I've been dead, and I know it's great to be alive. And for you to experience this necessity of the soul is the most important thing in this whole book.

Read the Bible. For every major turning point in my life, I have found the Bible to be a living book with a living message for me in key verses. Here are some of my turning-point verses so far: John 3:16 (receiving salvation), Philippians 4:13 (getting empowered), Philippians 3:14 (choosing a vocation), 1 Peter 5:7 (overcoming anxiety), and Ephesians 4:1 (continuing vocation). Right now the Bible is speaking to me from Psalms, Paul's epistles, and James.

When I once tried to point someone to the Bible, he responded, "Oh, I've already read the Bible." He didn't understand that reading the Bible once is not enough. The Bible is a dynamic book that speaks to our needs at each stage of life.

From my own experience, I know that reading the Bible in retirement is still a soul necessity.

Worship at church. After traveling or being away from church for a while, I miss it: the corporate worship of God, the hymns we sing, the friends we join hearts and hands with, the message the pastor brings. Now, I'm a big believer in private worship and the nourishment of solitude. I practice that on Godwin's Mountain, at home, and elsewhere. But nothing takes the place of church, for whom Jesus shed His blood (Acts 20:28). Yet, many retirees are tempted to give up on regular church attendance and participation. The Bible itself calls for us to be faithful to our convictions, our assembling together, and our encouragement of each other (Hebrews 10:23–25).

To be obedient to God, church remains a necessity instead of merely being an option (Ephesians 4:1–16). Further, we will find nourishment for the soul at church. In retirement, I find myself agreeing with Stéphane Mallarmé: "Every soul is a melody which needs renewing." Church is a source of soul renewal.

Pray everywhere. An old retiree stood in front of me as we waited in an appliance service line one day. He told me he offers a prayer of thanksgiving every morning when he wakes up and finds he's alive for a new day. I told him I do the same thing. He added, "It may not do any good, but it makes me feel better."

In recent years, I've often heard that kind of attitude about prayer. The idea seems to be that prayer affects our feelings and changes us but doesn't affect God. If you want a quick but good biblical treatment of that facet of prayer, you might read P. T. Forsyth's *The Soul of Prayer*. (You can find the complete text on the Internet.) In so many words, Forsyth said, "God has some blessings for us we'll never receive unless we ask for them." Both Jesus and James taught similar things about prayer.

In a public forum, a great Christian philosopher once testified about answered prayer in his own life. One of the doubters asked, "But couldn't all your answered prayers just be coincidences?"

The philosopher replied honestly, "Yes, but I find the coincidences come closer together when I pray."

Prayer may make us feel better, but the right quality of prayer may affect God's intentions toward us. For example, I've always heard people say that when it's your time to die, you're going to die. When your number is up, you're going. But that's not necessarily so.

In the Old Testament, King Hezekiah was sick and received God's word from Isaiah to set his house in order because he was going to die. Hezekiah wept bitterly and appealed to God in prayer. Before Isaiah got away, God directed him to turn around and give this response to Hezekiah: "I have heard thy prayer, I have seen thy tears: behold, I will heal thee. . . . And I will add unto thy days fifteen years" (2 Kings 20:5–6 KJV). And God did what He said He would.

Prayer is for all of life, at all times, and everywhere, but it is especially a necessity for the retirement soul. God can use our prayers to match our souls to each retirement stage of life. A platitude? No. As my own mother lay dying and spoke quietly with closed eyes, we would get close and ask her what she was saying. She would just reply, "Praying, praying, praying." She modeled dying as well as living.

God can help us accept what we can't change and what He chooses not to change. But God still chooses to answer prayers by stepping in to change lives and circumstances. Prayer is a retirement necessity of the soul.

I'm sure there are other necessities of the soul, but these necessities related to God and the spiritual life are essential for soul health. Otherwise—especially in retirement—disorders of the soul will likely occur.

DISORDERS OF THE SOUL

Retirement is an ideal time to get the soul in shape and bring harmony to the soul's discord. The Latin poet Horace wrote, "Why do you hasten to remove anything which hurts your eye, while if something affects your soul you postpone the cure until next year?" It is possible for the disordered soul to become ordered, but time is of the essence for retirees to make the change.

A number of years ago W. L. Northridge wrote a book titled *Disorders of the Emotional and Spiritual Life*. Among the disorders he wrote about are depression, jealousy, resentment, anxiety, martyr complex, critical spirit, and fear of old age.

Although these soul disorders can occur at any age or stage of life, retirees are particularly susceptible to them. Northridge concluded his book by saying that all the soul disorders he had written about can be cured only through a vital, spiritual experience. He wrote both as a trained psychologist and a pastor. The experiences of my life say amen to his conclusion.

A person can have the vital spiritual experience of being born again and still experience disorders of the soul, which are often reflected in the body. To keep a soul healthy, a person has to stay close to the Great Physician.

Since retirement is a time of backing off from required work and other things, it's also easy to back off from spiritual discipline and closeness to God. If we let that happen, our souls quickly get out of shape, and our minds tend to get out of order. Preventing disorders of the soul is best; but second best is returning to God, who alone can rightly order our souls and give us peace and rest.

BEING MAGNANIMOUS

Older people lean toward being sweet or sour, and the spiritual condition of their souls reflects which it is. Some of the sweetest, kindest people I know are older people with bad physical health and hard circumstances who seemingly are living in the dark night of the soul. Yet they choose to be great-souled, which is the literal meaning of *magnanimous*. They choose to spread sunshine rather than gloom. They themselves are a blessing.

To be magnanimous means to be generous, great-minded, greathearted, considerate, charitable, kind, forgiving, unselfish, and unspiteful. A magnanimous person is courageously noble in mind and heart. Such a person has a nature that is above petty feelings of hurt or jealousy, and the person does not hold a grudge. He is generous and kind in judging others and gives them the benefit of the doubt. In other words, a magnanimous person has a well-ordered soul.

Retirees can choose to be magnanimous. And they can choose to match their hearts and souls to great needs in a way that makes a positive difference. Or retirees can choose to be small-souled, small-minded, small-spirited, and self-centered.

One retired husband obviously had chosen this negative-gear approach for his regular behavior. His wife was a bit out of sorts one morning, and one of her friends asked, "Did you wake up gripey this morning?"

The woman replied, "No, I left him asleep in bed." No one enjoys being around petty, irritable, sour-souled people, whose very presence is a cloud on each day's sunshine.

Personally, I've been blessed by the magnanimous and pained by the small-souled. To choose to be magnanimous is to nourish your own soul and those of others, too. As Josiah Gilbert Holland said, "The soul, like the body, lives by what it feeds on." Feed on the blessing of being magnanimous.

SOUL ENRICHMENT

Firing up the soul. Ferdinand Foch said, "The most powerful weapon on earth is the human soul on fire." Jean de la Fontaine said, "Man is so made that when anything fires his soul impossibilities vanish." After the retirement euphoria is over, retirees may be in danger of flameout. Sometimes the spirit diminishes, and there is no fire in the bones, no sparkle in the eye, and no vision in the heart. The retired often need to be refired.

While retirees worry about outliving their money, many of them lose what makes life worth living: namely, the explosive power of a new affection. They lose purpose and challenge that give meaning to each day of life. They don't need busy work to fill up their time; they need meaning and worthwhile goals.

Staying interested. General Douglas MacArthur said, "Years may wrinkle the skin, but to give up interest wrinkles the soul." So what kinds of things can keep the inner person young while the outer person grows older? You might be expecting an answer of 101 things to keep you young in retirement. But that smacks of finding something to do to keep from being bored. And that kind of thing doesn't enrich the soul. Rather, giving ourselves to others is soul enriching.

Living within yourself. William Morrow said, "What lies behind us and what lies before us are tiny matters compared to what lies within us." In retirement, the facades and veneers of career life begin to fade, and we have to deal with who we really are, not just what we did to make a living.

As I mentioned earlier, if you ask many retirees who they are or what they do, they'll tell you what they used to do and what they used to be. That's not good enough. Each person always has more to write in the book of his life unless he lets his inner being die at retirement. So how does a person continue to grow the inner being, the soul, in retirement?

Every year—as I have since age twenty-nine—I still set new goals, and each day I write in my diary in green ink to remind me to keep on growing (God willing). I stay excited about life and what God wants me to do each day and each year.

The week before my dad died at age seventy-eight, he told me, "I try to learn something new every day." He was blind, but he listened to recorded books far into each night and shared in the daytime what he had learned the night before. Reading the Bible, the classics, biographies, magazines, and newspapers all keep a person from withdrawing his mind and letting it shrivel up in retirement.

For those willing to use computers, the Internet provides an almost inexhaustible wealth of information on any subject a person wants to learn and grow in. The important thing is to keep on using and stretching the mind, heart, soul, and spirit or else they will shrivel up like unused muscles. Use it or lose it.

Living beyond yourself. I told you how Dad learned each night and then shared with others what he had learned. That's another principle of soul enrichment: namely, living beyond self. I've known retirees who became reclusive, did away with their wristwatch, gave away or burned their dress clothes, and moved into the small shell of living only for self. That's mighty small-souled living. On the other hand, nothing enriches a soul like investing wisdom, experience, and resources in others.

As a retiree, I've taken in a lot of self-enjoyment from leisure-time activities: a cruise, foreign travel, smelling the coffee, socializing, and amusing myself with entertainment. But my greatest joys have come from living beyond myself and helping others. Without meaning to pat myself on the back, I'll simply list some of these joys, which may stir up ideas to help you live beyond yourself.

I have *mentored* younger or inexperienced people in writing, publishing, computing, splitting firewood, playing racquetball, and other skill areas. I have *ministered* by helping widows, neighbors, family members, and strangers. I have *encouraged* people around the world through e-mail and a newspaper column I've written. Churches have invited me to *share the gospel* as their interim pastor or supply preacher. And one highlight was *sharing a message of hope* with those in prison who had lost hope and seemed hungry to find it again.

Expressions of living beyond self might be quite different for you. But whatever your choices may be, it's important to live beyond self. The most miserable retirees I know are those who are wrapped up in themselves. The happiest ones I know live beyond themselves.

Before I began writing this chapter, here's what I read on a computer bulletin board for seniors: "I'm retiring in a month. Do you have any suggestions or ideas on how to stay busy?"

I replied that the right question is not how to stay busy; rather, it's how to stay *meaningfully busy*. Or to say it another way, retirees have the developmental task of learning how to enrich the soul. We're all novices to each new chapter of life, but we don't have to flounder in discovering how to enrich the soul. Living beyond self is one of the best ways to enrich the soul and grow older without getting old.

REFLECTIONS AND PROJECTIONS

- Recall what *soul* meant to you before you read this chapter; then reflect on any possible changes or additional meanings *soul* has taken on for you.
- How do the necessities of your soul match or differ from those I listed?
- What are you doing in retirement to enrich your soul?
- Consider one possession or maintenance you would like to downsize or delete.
- Prioritize three necessities of the soul you would choose for yourself.
- Choose one way you would like to enrich your inner being.
- Plan one way to mentor, help, or encourage someone else.
- Decide how you will commit to keep body and soul together in retirement.

RETIREMENT WORDS FROM THE WORD

Genesis 2:7; Matthew 22:37, 39; Luke 12:20; 2 Corinthians 4:16; 2 Corinthians 5:1; Philippians 3:13–14

PRAYER THOUGHTS

Father, thank You for making me a living soul and providing a body for both earth and heaven. Help me to see soul necessities as You do and to cooperate with You in overcoming disorders of my soul. May Your Spirit enrich my soul so that I will be a good steward of it both now and forever. Amen.

Chapter Nine

Ruts and Routines

*The only difference between a rut
and a grave is their dimensions.*

Ellen Glasgow

U pon retirement a person has the chance to reflect on how
he has lived life, to consider how he wants to live retirement life,
and to decide what to change and what not to change. While
there is the need for continuity in many areas of life, retirement
brings a special opportunity to break out of monotony and to
choose fresh, new ways to live life. Retirement can be a time to
get out of deadly ruts and to get into lively routines.

After the euphoria of retirement is over, after you get used
to not having an agenda, after you've gotten away from any
kowtowing to others, then it's time to consider the value of new
routines. So this chapter and the next one are about how to live
retirement life fruitfully and productively.

THE PROBLEM WITH RUTS

Literally, a rut is a deep track that wheels make in soft ground or wear in the ground over a period of time. Figuratively, a rut is a narrow, undeviating course of life or action. It's a deep groove of living life by habit.

So what's wrong with a rut? For those of us who have driven over rutted roads until we hit high center, we know what's wrong with ruts: getting stuck, going nowhere or only where others have gone, or going nowhere that's exciting or fresh. Since ruts show where others have gone, ruts may seem the safe furrow to follow; but for those willing to get out of the ruts, there is a big world out there.

Let me further underline what's wrong with the ruts of life. They are dull, monotonous, unrewarding, and unpromising. They are as boring as a treadmill, humdrum, unproductive, no fun, and have no passion or adventure in them. Ruts are so predictable that they take the wonder, excitement, and enthusiasm out of life. A rut is just a grave with both ends kicked out. That's the problem with ruts, but the problem is a curable one.

IDENTIFYING THE RUTS OF LIFE

Many retirees seem to categorically equate the ruts of life with whatever they've just retired from. That's a bit simplistic and unappreciative of what has gone on before retirement. Further, it's not nearly as helpful as some careful discernment between rigid ruts and productive routines.

Personally, I don't bad-mouth my career, and I would encourage others not to bad-mouth theirs. It's good to have a solid career and appreciate it for what it's worth. It pays the bills and enables retirement. It provides productive employment that usually includes gaining and using skills. In a work career we meet and make friends who become a part of us for most of our lives or all of our lives. In work we find meaning and fulfillment. Any honorable work matched up with a person's interest and potential is a worthy way to spend a large part of life. But when a career ends and retirement comes, it's time to sort out old ruts and choose new paths that are enjoyable, fruitful, and helpful—and may even include a new career. Retirement shouldn't lead to a dead end or an idling existence.

There are some clues to help us identify ruts we need to break out of. For example, a middle-aged friend of mine spent over half his life in one corporate job and then chose to take on another rather mundane job as a profitable hobby. When we talked about it, my friend said, "Johnnie, I just burned out in my regular job. So I decided to retire from it and do my side job full time." Though there was nothing wrong with his career job, the years of rigid repetition caused him to feel he was in a rut. In such a case, Ernest Renan's counsel might be the retirement solution: "Relax yourself from one job by doing a different one."

However, many people work right up to retirement and enjoy their jobs without experiencing burnout. Where I used to work, one veteran would encourage new employees in hard times by saying, "This is a very unusual year." Then he would add, "But I've worked here twenty-five years, and so far every year has been unusual." When I came to retirement from the same corporation, I could agree that every year had been unusual and interesting: a mix of good times and hard times, successes and failures, joys and sorrows, but not burnout. Despite fully enjoying my career, at retirement I was able to identify ruts and semiruts that I wanted to get out of, and I've pretty much done that.

Commuting was a rut. Every day on the interstate had become a rat race around an obstacle course of construction. Most everyone on the road drove faster or slower than I wanted them to, and through signs and gestures, they also let me know that I was driving faster or slower than they wanted me to.

Corporate budgeting had become a rut game to me each year as I tried to outguess the economy and build on shifting corporate strategies. I was a "suit" but felt more comfortable in jeans or shorts. When I began my career in publishing, I enjoyed the excitement of travel: flying in jets, staying in good hotels, renting cars newer than what I owned, eating meals included in my expense account, and meeting with lots of interesting people.

But over time, I grew weary of traveling, eating where they didn't have cornbread, and only being with my family by phone a lot of nights. I did love my work; but when it came time to retire, I didn't have any trouble identifying the ruts I was getting out of and the new life I was moving into: a life of time with family, sleeping on my own bed and pillow, and commuting in jeans from my bedroom to a home office a few feet away. For me, career was the main meal, but retirement became its dessert.

AVOIDING RETIREMENT RUTS

The tiresome rut. Ruts can be as much a part of retirement as they were preretirement. In fact, some people retire tired, and they themselves are tiresome to others. These people tend to carry their ruts with them at each age and stage of life. G. K. Chesterton put it this way: "Woe unto them that are tired of everything, for everything will certainly be tired of them."

George Bernard Shaw counseled, "Better keep yourself clean and bright; you are the window through which you must see the world."

Some honest self-appraisal can help a person change from being a personal rut himself. True friends willing to risk their friendship can also help a person change from being a personal rut. This challenge fits in with Ellen Glasgow's observation: "The toughest kind of mountain climbing is getting out of a rut." Someone else said, "He who lives in a rut will always be narrow."

It's critically important for a person to know he's in a tiresome rut if he needs to make changes for retirement to be life's best chapter. Voltaire said, "The secret of being tiresome is to tell everything." Perhaps the secret to getting out of the rut of being tiresome is to tell only in part and to listen completely as a good conversationalist. As Benjamin Franklin grew older, he set a personal goal of listening more and speaking less. Besides, when a person is quick to hear and slow to speak, what he does say can go through his mind and heart before it comes out of his mouth. And that's good.

The past-tense rut. Although retirees have lived most of their lives in the past, it is wise not to camp in that memory rut too long at a time. In Europe I've seen a lot of old cathedrals, castles, and other structures with scaffolding around them and what seems like constant repair going on. Phyllis and I became so amused with this fact that we began a collection of scaffolding pictures that include Big Ben in London, St. Basil's in Moscow, and other famous sites.

When we began to take the scaffolding pictures, it occurred to me that there's often more effort to maintain the past than to prepare for the future. I know the value of heritage and history and preserving memories. But retirees will do well not to allow themselves to fall into the trap of past-tense living at the expense of the present and the future. If we find ourselves living and talking mostly about the past, we're likely not doing what we should to live in the present and plan for the future.

The reclusive rut. At times people who have had lots of good interpersonal relationships and friends seem to enter retirement as if it were a license to become a recluse or a hermit. They may get rid of their suits or work clothes, abandon interaction with former friends, and burn bridges between all past relationships and the present.

If a retiree makes this choice, he chooses a new kind of rut—a rut that truly is a type of grave that isolates him from caring for others or being cared for by others. No matter how well a person may have written the chapters of his life to the point of retirement, to choose the reclusive rut is to end life as an incomplete novel—or an unfinished symphony. Ending life in such a rut is to abandon stewardship of life while still being held accountable for it.

FROM RUTS TO ROUTINES

Ruts and routines share repetition and some other characteristics but are quite different. Although dictionaries tend to blur the differences between ruts and routines, I'm using *routine* in its most positive sense, which is far different from a rut and much more exciting, enjoyable, and productive.

Among other things, a routine is a consistent, regular, patterned way of doing things. A routine procedure provides a dependable route to a particular destination or result. It is a planned, organized course of action. In the world of computers, a routine is a set of coded instructions that directs the computer to perform specific tasks for effective results. A rut deadens, but a routine enables. Flannery O'Connor said, "Routine is a condition of survival." Retirees need a set of well-thought-out routines that match what they want retirement living to be.

More than being a condition of survival, routine is a requirement for productive retirement and stewardship of life.

RETAINING REWARDING ROUTINES

Alfred Edward Perlman wrote, "After you've done a thing the same way for two years, look it over carefully. After five years, look at it with suspicion. And after ten years, throw it away and start all over." That's good advice for discovering ruts and getting out of them, but it's not good advice for beneficial routines.

When the retiree is suddenly freed from having to work for a living, he may revert to childish irresponsibility or adolescent anarchy and give up valuable routines as well as the ruts of life. I'll mention just a few examples to show the need for retirees to retain good routines—even if the routines do need some evaluation and improvement.

Hold on to good hygiene. In work life, a person usually has some regular cycle for bathing, grooming, and taking care of health needs. That routine needs to continue, but retirement provides both the interruption and the temptation to get sloppy in hygiene. A retiree's memory of how long it's been since he bathed may become a problem. My regular workout at the downtown YMCA used to trigger a daily shower; now I have to remind myself to shower between Saturday nights or often enough to need to change towels two or three times a week.

Most of us will not receive the candid criticism a woman gave one famous grammarian. She said, "You smell!"

His retort was, "No, madam, I stink; you smell."

Perhaps it was a retiree who said, "Instead of taking baths, I've decided to stay away from people." Even hermits owe it to themselves to bathe regularly.

Company-provided physicals and eye and dental insurance may be a thing of the past for retirees, but the regular monitoring of health should not be a thing of the past. (Refer to chapter 7, "Body and. . .") Brushing teeth, combing hair, and watching one's weight ought to continue to be both a routine and a want-to in life for both health and appearance. Unfortunately, some retirees just let themselves go to pot in every way.

Keep on exercising. Retirement is a crisis point in maintaining or beginning an exercise routine. Newly retired friends of ours stepped up their exercise, selectively altered their diet, and lost a generation of pounds. They look great and say they feel good. They were health conscious before retirement but disciplined themselves at retirement and moved up a notch or two in taking care of themselves. They had a petty good routine before retirement but improved it.

When I retired, I kept on doing all the exercise routine I did before except for changing some jogging to brisk walking with Phyllis. Although I don't believe everything I read, a good source stated that older people can maintain their aerobic capacity and still lose significant upper body strength if they don't mix in some weight training. So I added light weights to my exercise routine and upped my sit-ups from thirty to fifty a day. As a sports doctor told me one time about our exercise routines, "We may not live any longer, but our quality of life will be better." I believe he was right, and exercise has paid off for me.

It's a matter of chagrin that clothes tend to shrink more quickly in the average retiree's closet than during preretirement days. Living closer to the fridge may be part of the problem. A stash of junk foods in a drawer or closet may compound the problem. Also, with more optional time and less responsibility, retirees can find themselves couch potatoes more than they are participators. John F. Kennedy said, "We must use time as a tool, not a couch."

A young woman I know is related to parents and in-laws who are approximately the same age. One of the couples has faithfully kept an exercise routine through the years; the other couple has not. I heard the young woman comment that the exercisers are like teenagers compared to the other couple who haven't exercised. The thing that makes exercise a routine instead of a rut is the payoff in quality of life and perhaps in length of life. It is quickening rather than deadening. And it's even a good idea to vary and spice up one's exercise routine.

Continue to value your values. The heritage of our parents begins to instill values in us from birth through adolescence and beyond. Then we choose our own values to go with those we've inherited. Upon retirement, there is often the temptation to reduce the priority we place on our values. This reduction in values may include everything from spiritual values to those of citizenship and the integrity of personhood. Before retirement, the way we expressed our values involved routines that are invaluable and need to be continued.

Church attendance, Bible reading, stewardship of money, good citizenship, neighborliness, and good commitment in marriage are just a few of the values expressed through routines. Yet these are some of the same expressions of values that often begin to get short shrift upon retirement. John Spaulding wrote, "Keep yourself alive by throwing day by day fresh currents of thought and emotion into the things you have come to do from habit." And surely this counsel is needed most in the field of values.

CHOOSING PURPOSE-FILLED ROUTINES

Wise people prepare financially for retirement because they hope they'll have a long life, and they know it will take a lot of money to live on. Many of those same people don't realize how much time they will have on their hands when they retire and don't consider the need for new, purposeful routines to make their lives both enjoyable and productive. Aimless retirees may become like water that seeks its own level. They lack destination, purpose, goals, discipline, and the empowerment of making new decisions and acquiring needed skills.

Your retirement destinations. There is a joy sometimes in being a happy wanderer without a specific destination, and that's fine. However, think of retirement destinations as specific purposes or goals—even happy wandering—for this stage of life. Then consider purpose-filled routines as the methods and routes you will use in the days, months, and years to reach your retirement destinations.

At any stage in retirement, when a person doesn't have destinations and chosen routines, he becomes somewhat like Alice in Wonderland (Lewis Carroll, *Alice's Adventures in Wonderland*):

> *"Would you tell me, please, which way I ought to go from here?"* Alice asked.
> *"That depends a good deal on where you want to get to,"* said the Cheshire Cat.

"I don't much care where," said Alice.

"Then it doesn't matter which way you go," said the Cat.

We all exchange each day of life for something, and it is a prostitution of life to exchange it for something unworthy of our potential and our calling. José Ortega y Gasset wrote, "Life is lost at finding itself all alone. Mere egoism is a labyrinth. . . . Really to live is to be directed toward something, to progress toward a goal" (*The Revolt of the Masses*). Louis Kronenberger further defined our problem when he wrote, "The trouble with our age is that it is all signpost and no destination" (*Company Manners*).

Getting your act together. One retirement irony is the complaint of being too busy and not having enough time. This retirement cliché usually comes with a smile and the implication that busyness is what retirement is all about. However, I would counsel retirees to choose purpose-filled routines that will keep them from feeling like Egyptian mummies (you know: pressed for time). The cycles of work life have built-in routines, but retirement calls for rearranging and reorganizing how we go about the chosen and unchosen tasks of living.

More simply, retirement is a time to choose good, new habits rather than let yourself continue or fall into bad old habits. Horace Bushnell wrote, "Habits are to the soul what the veins and arteries are to the blood, the courses in which it moves." Hesiod wrote, "It is best to do things systematically since we are only human, and disorder is our worst enemy." Napoleon I said, "Order marches with weighty and measured strides; disorder is always in a hurry." And the Bible commands, "Let all things be done decently and in order" (1 Corinthians 14:40 KJV).

In retirement there is time for both the destination of

happy spontaneity and the destination of powerful productivity through routines of purpose and organization.

BURNING BRIGHTLY ONCE AGAIN

Retirement occurs for many stated reasons: reaching a specific age, personal health problems, family member health problems, downsizing, bankrupt companies, personal choice at any age, or even the expected relatively brief careers such as those of professional athletes, who tend to retire in their thirties. Like lightbulbs, most careers have a life expectancy that ends and calls for a replacement or renewal.

Despite stated reasons for retirement, burnout is often an accompanying factor involved in retirement. (Interestingly, *burnout* entered English in 1940 and *retiree* in 1945.) Burnout refers to the condition of being worn-out physically or emotionally because of long-term stresses and demands that exhaust a person's total being. The light that once burned so brightly now burns dimly or smolders in burnout. For the burned-out person, life has become dingy, dark, or stale and isn't any fun—or not nearly as much fun as it once was.

The Bible has a word of hope for those who are bruised and burned out. Isaiah 42:3 (NIV) says, "A bruised reed he will not break, and a smoldering wick he will not snuff out." The NRSV translation reads, "A bruised reed he will not break, and a dimly burning wick he will not quench." If you will let Him, God will heal your bruises. He will trim the burned-out wick, refill the lamp with His oil, and cause the light of your life to burn brightly once again.

Not too long ago I learned the word *quotidian*. It simply

refers to things that recur daily—such as sunrises and sunsets. A lot of life is repetitious, and we ought not despise the quotidian cycles that give us a sense of order and comfort. At the same time, we ought to be open to new experiences, challenging goals, serendipities, and what old theologians used to refer to as "the expulsive power of a new affection." In short, it's good to know the difference between ruts and routines and to be willing to explore the road less traveled—or even to make a new road.

REFLECTIONS AND PROJECTIONS

- What are three enduring appreciations you have for your work career?
- Identify at least two preretirement work ruts you're glad to be out of.
- How happy are you with the routines or habits you've gotten into since you retired?
- What one recurring retirement attitude, feeling, or action would you most like to change? Label it, record a date by which the change will have occurred, and map out the routine you plan to use to make the change.
- Choose three destinations or goals you would most like to reach in retirement. (For example, a place to visit, a dream to fulfill, a good habit to form.) Let G-O-A-L become your retirement acronym: a goal-oriented approach to life.

RETIREMENT WORDS FROM THE WORD

Ecclesiastes 3:1; Ecclesiastes 12:13; Matthew 25:18; James 4:17; 2 Thessalonians 3:13; Matthew 5:14, 16

PRAYER THOUGHTS

Father, thank You for the gift of work. Thank You for delivering us from unproductive ruts that deaden the spirit and fail to provide good stewardship of life. Help us to realize that retirement is not a time to bury our talents in a hole or to fail to do the good You've revealed to us. Refresh our desire to do good and form right habits. Trim the wicks of our lives so that our light will shine more brightly and glorify Your name. Amen.

CHAPTER TEN

WHILE IT IS DAY

We all exchange each day of life for something.

JOHNNIE GODWIN

When former talk-show host Johnny Carson was asked what he would like for his epitaph, Carson replied, "I'll be right back." When we have exchanged retirement and all the days of our lives for something, we won't be right back (unless the Lord comes back first). The Bible underlines this fact by saying, "We must work the works of him who sent me while it is day; night is coming when no one can work" (John 9:4 NRSV). So far, all those who have died have gone ahead; no one has been left behind.

We all exchange each day of life for something, and retirement doesn't change this fact. So how we choose to spend the days of our retirement reflects the values we hold and what we're willing to exchange life for. Ultimately, commitment to Christ and obeying Him is the only thing worth exchanging our lives for (see Matthew 16:24–27).

Given that foundational truth, we have opportunities and

challenges to exchange the days of our lives in a timely way for every God-designed activity for each season of life. Retirees can especially be glad God wants us to be happy and enjoy ourselves both in work and play (see Ecclesiastes 3:1–15).

So far, I have purposely avoided writing a book titled *Things to Do in Retirement*. Rather, I've mostly chosen to share my personal pilgrimage, observations, and tips for you to consider how to customize retirement to suit yourself. My purpose still isn't to provide a catalog of things to choose to do in retirement. However, in talking about how to spend the days and years of retirement life, I will focus on a few specific possibilities you might find helpful as you choose how to exchange the days of your life.

The possibilities I'll mention may just be a catalyst that causes your mind to unleash new retirement destinations and routines for yourself. After all, one purpose of books I write is to get people to think for themselves. Your personhood and your experiences blend together to make you unique—one of a kind. So let what I suggest stimulate you to choose how you want to be useful and productive in ways that best fit you. But now, here's some specific counsel.

Make It a Habit to Help Others

In my neighborhood, I've become known as the local Paul Bunyan. Our neighborhood has a lot of trees that vary from large to huge, and each time we have a storm, it tends to fell some trees or at least blow off some large limbs. One of my hobbies for twenty-three years has been cutting and splitting my own firewood (ever since we bought fifty-six acres on a Tennessee ridge and named it Godwin's Mountain). So in retirement I routinely offer to help cut up fallen trees and carry them away in my pickup to Godwin's Mountain—or to some needy soul.

I'm small of stature, and one of my neighbors, Don Slepski, is a large but gentle man who is soft spoken. When a storm felled several of his trees, I cut them up, and he loaded the logs and limbs onto my pickup. After we did that for the better part of two days, Don—who wears a hat that says *Think Big*—said, "Johnnie, you're Paul Bunyan, and I'm Babe the Blue Ox."

I liked hearing that comparison. And I've enjoyed becoming a Good Samaritan who helps people at the side of the road instead of a professional passerby about to be late for work or a meeting.

Usually retired people are experienced and skilled in one or more areas of expertise and can freely offer specialized help to those who need it. For example, one hundred high-school students signed up for Latin, but the Latin teacher had just retired and left a vacancy the school hadn't been able to fill. A seventy-eight-year-old great-grandmother had taught Latin for twenty-seven years before she retired at sixty-one.

But when this teaching emergency arose, she was glad to bring her Latin expertise back into the classroom until the school could find another qualified teacher. Like an oak tree that retains its leaves through the winter until a new generation takes over, retirees can bridge generations of knowledge and skills.

Other kinds of help needed don't require any special training other than opening your eyes and committing to help. A retiree can house-sit for friends or neighbors on vacation, provide transportation for those who need it, help someone with their children, and all the other ways to help that come to mind. As retirees are useful and productive, they can help others and also continue to find personal fulfillment.

Volunteer for Something

Retiree Copper Daugherty, one of my best friends, was diagnosed with lung cancer and cured of it a few years ago. When he got well, he did more than thank those who had helped him. He volunteered as a part of his weekly routine to help several days a week in the cancer clinic, where he has empathy with those who are getting treated. He has happily alternated that routine with playing golf, ministering through his church, being a helpful grandparent, and carrying out other routines that give special meaning to his retirement life.

Those who want to volunteer don't usually have to be asked; they take the initiative in finding helpful and meaningful ways to meet needs of others. Some volunteers deliver meals to nourish and enable those who can't prepare their own food but still want to live in their own homes.

Others take audiocassettes of books or sermons to those who are confined to home but want to grow and stay lively as long as they live. Special support groups or ministries need volunteers to stand by a phone line to offer support, encouragement, or prayers for those who call in. Mentoring formally or informally is a great gift retirees have to offer those who are younger or need help in developing skills, knowledge, attitudes, and actions. With wisdom and experience, retirees are well suited for this kind of helpfulness.

Volunteering for mission assignments is a Good News–sharing experience that enriches retirees and those they go on mission to. I read about missionary Margaret Burks's work in Africa when she was eighty-four years old. She is just one of thousands of retirees who have taken their Christian witness and a variety of skills to people who need both.

Volunteer mission assignments may be weeks, months, or a

couple of years, but God can use these laser-beamed volunteer efforts to etch His will into eternity. How do you get started? Share your willingness with your pastor, local church, or denominational mission board. Then you will enter a great adventure.

ADOPT A PROJECT-ORIENTED APPROACH TO RETIREMENT

Over the dozen years of my retirement, I've discovered I don't like to commit myself to long-term projects. That gets to be too much like preretirement work and not enough like retirement. I meditate and pray over opportunities. Then I decide. So when I say yes to something, I do it wholeheartedly and without resentment, and when I say no to something, I decline the invitation without guilt.

The value of a project-oriented approach to retirement is that it calls for a degree of commitment, work, goals, and results, but it is usually for a short term. The project may be like a day trip, a cruise, or a longer journey, but it is still relatively short compared to all of life. A project-oriented approach allows a person to be productive but flexible and not get bogged down in preretirement ruts. Retirees can be useful in some way until they're used up and have to become care-receivers themselves. Even then there may be ways they can help others.

KEEP A RETIREMENT JOURNAL

I started keeping a daily diary when I was sixteen years old and still keep one today. However long or short the years of retirement are, a diary or journal is a valuable tool for many reasons.

It's still true that the dimmest ink is stronger than the strongest memory. And memory doesn't tend to be a strong suit in the retirement years. So a diary or journal is a good record book to check for facts and to retain wonderful experiences that our minds may no longer be able to recall.

Further, retirement can be a lot more productive if you set measurable goals, record them in a journal, and note your progress or completion of those goals. Phyllis and I weigh ourselves daily and record the weight in a diary. This monitoring tends to keep our weight from ballooning up. The journal is a good monitor for other health matters, too, such as recording blood pressure, results of visits to doctors, and other medical information.

A retirement journal can help retirees keep track of what they're exchanging these days of their lives for. It can help us measure real retirement against retirement dreams or goals. In this way, a daily diary can be a tool to help remind us of the goals we've set and to what degree the day we spent moved toward the goals we've set. Goals may be for a year, five years, or ten years (but remember to always add *Deo volente*—God willing—to the goals).

Although my diary would be a good sedative to induce sleep, I like to think it contains matters of heritage and values family members might profit from reading. And what better place could you find to record the grand sayings and antics of your grandchildren?

As I reread my diaries, I get a sense of who I was, who I became, who I'm becoming, and who I would like to become. I saw a hardback journal on sale for $2.99. You may pay more for a journal, but the investment is worth the money if you'll get one and begin the discipline of keeping a daily journal. Or if you prefer to work on a computer, there are a number of software programs to help you keep a diary or journal. Try a diary for, say, a month; you may like it, and it may make a contribution to your retirement life and productivity.

MAKE A DAILY TO-DO LIST

I know I said we retirees don't want a daily agenda (see the section in chapter 5 titled "The Agenda Question"), but that was at the first stage of retirement. Things change, and we change in retirement. It's kind of fun to list ten things to do today and then productively cross the items off one at a time—or move some of the items to a new to-do list. On the other hand, because you're retired, you can just smile and throw the list in the wastebasket at the end of the day if you want to.

On the worthwhile side, one writer noted that just making a to-do list causes a person to be about 20 percent more productive than not making one. Whatever the increase in productivity percentage might be, I find that I get more done if I make a to-do list.

So I have the habit of making a daily or weekly to-do list. That habit leads me to do some useful things I would otherwise leave undone. Further, most things that don't make it to my to-do list are out of sight and out of memory. I might mention that most of the items on my to-do list are want-to's and not have-to's. And that includes Phyllis's *honey-please* items instead of *honey-do* items.

DARE TO REACH YOUR POTENTIAL

Benjamin Franklin retired from his first career of being a printer in 1748 at age forty-two, which turned out to be precisely the midpoint of his life. Although he always liked to refer to himself as a printer, it was in the second half of his life that he pursued a variety of careers for which he became famous. Most notably, in the second half of his life, he became the only person to sign all four founding papers of our nation: the Declaration of Independence, the treaty with France, the peace accord with Britain, and the Constitution.

Instead of looking upon retirement as the peak of one's career, dare to let it be a mountaintop that enables you to envision even greater accomplishments and careers in retirement. Too old for that? Oh, no. Consider examples of those who achieve some of their greatest accomplishments in their senior years.

Handel composed *Messiah* when he was fifty-six. Victor Hugo published *Les Miserables* at sixty. Jacques Offenbach wrote his ninetieth operetta at sixty-one. At sixty-two Agatha Christie turned her story of "Three Blind Mice" into *The Mousetrap*, which still holds the record for the longest continuous run of a play at one theater. At sixty-six Boris Pasternak completed *Doctor Zhivago*.

At seventy William Wordsworth climbed a local peak and came down with new sonnets in his head. At seventy-eight Renoir kept painting despite being confined to a wheelchair by rheumatoid arthritis.

At eighty George Bernard Shaw gave up driving but continued to walk up to six miles at a stretch. At eighty-one Henri Matisse completed his decoration of a Dominican chapel. At eighty-two Goethe completed his masterpiece, *Faust*. At eighty-three Horowitz played the piano in Carnegie Hall. At eighty-five Carl Sandburg published *Honey and Salt*. At eighty-six Robert Frost recited at John F. Kennedy's presidential inauguration. At eighty-seven Picasso began a new series of etchings. At eighty-eight Arthur Rubinstein gave twelve piano concerts in America and fifteen in Europe. At eighty-nine Georgia O'Keeffe began a new series of oil paintings.

At ninety Andres Segovia played over fifty concerts on his classical guitar. At ninety-one Frank Lloyd Wright continued work on the Marin County government center and several other projects. At age ninety-two P. G. Wodehouse bemoaned the fact that he had taken up golf too late because he had been fooling around writing stories and things. At ninety-three Pablo Casals continued to begin each day playing two Bach preludes and fugues on the piano. At ninety-four Shaw released his final work for publication. At ninety-five jazz pianist Eubie Blake played for a celebration on the White House lawn. At ninety-six Bertrand Russell wrote his final diatribe against religion. At ninety-seven Marc Chagall continued to paint and oversee his own business affairs. At ninety-eight Irving Berlin refused to let the ASCAP (music association) honor him with a full-page advertisement in the *New York Times*. At ninety-eight Eubie Blake was still accepting paying gigs. And, in a way, George Burns and Bob Hope did their last gigs after turning one hundred.

LEARN NEW TRICKS
TO GO WITH THE OLD ONES

The cliché says that you can't teach an old dog new tricks. Well, first of all, we're humans and not dogs. Second, I suspect an old dog could learn new tricks if he wanted to. Further, besides what you've already read, history is full of examples of people who learned or did new things at retirement age.

I was retired at fifty-five, which was the same age that Mark Twain learned to ride a bicycle. At fifty-eight John Steinbeck set out in a camper to discover America, which led him to write *Travels with Charlie* and win the Nobel Prize with it. At age fifty-nine Daniel Defoe's first novel, *Robinson Crusoe*, was published.

At sixty-four Dr. Samuel Johnson began a walking tour of Scotland and the isles off its western coast. At sixty-nine John Cage presented *A House Full of Music* using eight hundred schoolchildren. At seventy-one Henry Miller churned out 115 watercolors in five months for charitable contributions. At seventy-two Dizzy Gillespie made his debut as a dramatic actor. Although William Carlos Williams was a medical doctor for over forty years, at age seventy-four he completed his best-known poem, *Paterson.*

At seventy-six Grandma Moses gave up embroidery because of arthritis and began to paint. At seventy-nine she had her first show of art in New York City. At one hundred Grandma Moses went back to work and completed twenty-five more paintings.

For those over one hundred: The Delany sisters published a book about their first one hundred years and then wrote a follow-up volume.

On a personal note, with much less grandeur than what you've just read, I've taken up a few new things in my retirement. I researched vacuum cleaners, bought a good one, and became a skilled vacuumer. I got on the Internet and became an amateur travel expert—using the term *expert* loosely.

Although writing and publishing made up the primary context for my work career, at retirement I had never realized my dream of writing a newspaper column. In retirement, I wrote "Words and Things," a weekly column for the Gannett chain of newspapers for nine years. Writing the newspaper column seemed to hone, sharpen, and groove my writing skills. A goal not yet reached is my ambition to play a harmonica well enough that others can recognize the tunes. So far, I play only a poor rendition of "When the Saints Go Marching In," and that's with the help of a book with numbers for the notes.

Marie von Ebner-Eschenbach said, "You will stay young as long as you learn, form new habits, and don't mind being contradicted." I would add the ingredient of curiosity. The curious never get bored to death, and they reveal that youth is more a matter of the heart than a matter of the calendar.

But to get real experience into the picture, let's read what Sarah and Elizabeth Delany had to say when they were 105 and 103: "Most folks think getting older means giving up, not trying anything new. Well, we don't agree with that. As long as you can see each day as a chance for something new to happen, something you never experienced before, you will stay young" (*The Delany Sisters' Book of Everyday Wisdom*).

CONSIDER GETTING AND USING A COMPUTER

You may already have a computer since seniors are among the fastest-growing groups getting computers and doing e-mail and the Internet. Or I may just have turned you off with this suggestion. With my awareness of how negative a lot of people feel about the idea of using a computer, I was going to leave out this suggestion.

But the potential for enriching your retirement through a computer is too great to dismiss. Someone you trust can make the buying decision for you if you don't care to, and you can buy all you need for one thousand dollars or under. That includes the computer, monitor, and printer. A family member, friend, or someone else can set the thing up to do what it's supposed to do if you don't want to try it yourself.

Then your basic learning curve calls for flipping on a switch, pressing on a plastic thing called a mouse, and pointing an arrow at little symbols you click on. Typing? Hunt-and-peck will do. Oh, there's a little more to it than that, but not too much.

Here are some of the values of owning a computer and learning just a few basics: You can send and get e-mail immediately from family, friends, and people all over the world—assuming they have a computer, too, of course. It's quicker and cheaper than regular postal mail. You can read or write e-mail any time of the day or night. You can quickly research information on anything of interest to you, check the stock market, get sports schedules and scores, look at weather forecasts, print coupons for discounts, balance your bank account, pay bills, do your Christmas card list, or just about anything else you want to do.

The former president of my corporation excitedly called me—some time after we had both been downsized—and said, "Johnnie, did you get my e-mail?" I told him not yet and asked when he sent it. He said, "About ten minutes ago. It was my first e-mail, and it will be a miracle if you get it." I got it. But it was a smiler that he who had been president over thousands was so proud that he himself had begun a new skill.

Another one of my with-it friends had dragged his feet on getting a fax machine during corporate days and even an answering machine to receive messages from family and friends in retirement. Then one day I checked my e-mail and received this message: "Hello, Johnnie. We decided to get with the now-generation. We got a new computer and are able to e-mail." He and his wife had joined the large percentage of adults over fifty who have a computer in their home to have online access. My friend had reason to be as proud as Punch, and I enjoy hearing from him regularly.

The late Ralph Grubbs, my dear friend, was visually and otherwise physically impaired. He was blind in one eye and had trouble seeing out of the other eye. He had had cancer, a heart attack, and diabetes; but he could work computer circles around anyone else I knew. When I was Ralph's interim pastor, I offered a general challenge during a Bible study. Ralph told me that challenge was what got him started using his computer and printer for a snail-mail ministry of cards to people who were homebound, in crisis, or just having a birthday. Later, when he got a "real" pastor, he accepted the challenge to put all the church records on computer. The last time I saw Ralph, he was dying with cancer; but he hadn't quit living until he quit breathing and entered a better life by far.

Enough of the hard-sell approach on computers. I'm aware that some retiree friends of mine no longer even wear a watch. Some of them refuse to answer a ringing telephone and don't want a machine that faxes or answers or computes in their house or life. So a final word about computers: Do it if you want to; don't if you don't want to. That's a large part of what retirement is about. (But, lightheartedly, let me say shame on you if you don't compute.)

DRESS UP ONCE OR TWICE A WEEK

In the big scope of things, this is a small retirement suggestion but a worthy one. I exchanged the habit of wearing suits and neckties every day for casual clothes. So have some of my friends. In fact, the wife of one of my friends complains often that all her husband wears now is grubbies. It pleases him to wear grubbies most of the time—as he works in the yard and grubs in the dirt—but his routine of grubbiness bothers her.

Although I'm biased to vote for grubbies, I still dress up for church or special occasions. And I dress up a bit when I follow my routine of taking Phyllis on a date each week. Even in retirement, it's good for both you and others to know that you can still "clean up pretty good." Retirees don't need to impress anyone, but it's nice both to know and show you can still look nice.

MAKE FRIENDSHIPS A PRIORITY

Some of my best friendships go back more than fifty years, and I cherish their golden nature. I make it a point to try to keep those friendships in good repair with calls, cards, and occasional get-togethers or visits. I believe it's important not to retire your friendships when you retire. Despite best promises to stay in touch with those you've worked beside or lived among, retirement calls for special efforts to keep long-term friendships alive and healthy.

Some of my best friendships go back less than two years, and some of those friends are a lot younger than fifty years old. They're baby boomers or generation X-ers, or the next generation as well as those of my own era. One of the well-known factors for successful retirement is making new friends of all ages—having intergenerational friendships.

I've found that real friendships are gender-proof and age-proof. In retirement, I did contract work within a woman's organization on two different occasions. I was one of a handful of men there and about the only retiree around. Yet I didn't sense any female chauvinism toward me and found a world of new friends. I mentored them, and they mentored me; now some time removed from that work, these new friends and I still stay in touch.

Retirement put me twenty-five miles away from the site of my daily work and YMCA racquetball friends, so I mostly gave up racquetball except for occasionally beating a ball against the wall at our local church's racquetball court. Then one night I got a call from a guy named Lynn McFarlin. In short, Lynn said, "Johnnie, you don't know me. I'm Lynn McFarlin. I just moved to town from Texas, heard you play racquetball, and wondered if you would like to play in the morning."

When I asked how old he was and how long he had been playing, I learned he was the age of my oldest son, and I was twenty years older. He had been playing racquetball for about twenty years, and so had I. So we got together and played and became fast friends. We mostly alternated in beating each other at racquetball, but both of our families won in our newfound friendship. That friendship continues even today, though Dr. McFarlin and his family moved back to Texas, where he's on the staff of the Cooper Aerobics Center Clinic. And now I'm playing racquetball with another young friend named Mark McDaniel. He's good!

Dr. Jia Yang is professor of English at the University of Beijing. She is young enough to be my daughter but teaches PhD candidates in China and is internationally recognized for leadership of those who are visually impaired. Jia herself is legally blind but manages well with the help of a computer and other tools. We have met face-to-face only once—when I headed up a Christian publishers exhibit at the 1996 Beijing International Book Fair. The time we shared in 1996 was just a few minutes but still long enough for me to learn of her visual impairment and for me to tell her that my mother was legally blind, too. Then Jia asked for my e-mail address.

A month later I was surprised to get my first e-mail from her; but since then, we have exchanged hundreds of e-mails and have become good friends. One joy for me was to e-mail Jia my weekly "Words and Things" and get her feedback. Over a period of time, Jia began to use my newspaper columns in her English classes. And one year she prepared a supplementary textbook from them to be used with over one thousand PhD candidates at the University of Beijing.

The most important thing we share is friendship. But out of that friendship, she has seen potential in my meager efforts and multiplied them with her own efforts in a way that I never could have by myself. Friendship is partnership in the great journey of life.

These are just a few examples of new friendships I've made in retirement. One of the interesting things is that I didn't meet these new friends while I was just hanging around the house and wondering what to do in retirement. I was out and about, wanting to make new friends and live life fully.

As you move on in retirement, you'll discover that you go to more funerals and fewer weddings. About the only consolation in this change is that funerals don't require a wedding shower or rehearsal. The sad thing is that many lifelong or career-long friends die. Besides the grief of losing friends and retaining only gratitude for their lives, your friendship circle grows ever smaller—*unless you make new friends and some younger friends.*

Friendships old and new can be among the richest and most rewarding parts of a productive retirement. They cause a person to look beyond self and focus on others. Friends help a person overcome the misery and enslavement of selfish living that monopolizes conversations, thoughts, and resources. So always be on the lookout for new friends. Begin by getting their name and giving yours; then let friendship flourish as it will.

ANOTHER APPROACH TO RETIREMENT

Good friend and former colleague Howard Foshee has led seminars on retirement. Besides that, he's well into his second decade of retirement (or semiretirement) and practicing what he's taught. Howard and his wife, Zola, are in the midst of a rich and productive retirement, which hasn't come about as an accident. Rather, it came from convictions, planning, and carried-out actions.

Although Howard loved his job, he approached retirement with an awareness that it wasn't his life and that he was about to begin a new phase of life called retirement. He and Zola wanted that phase to continue to include growing, learning, giving, and finding what God had for them in retirement. Their want-to challenged them to plan retirement rather than just let it happen to them.

Here's what they recommend:

Develop a mission statement. This statement is a purposeful effort to get at who you want to be after retirement—instead of spending retirement in a "has-been" mode. The statement includes what you want to contribute, what your foundational principles and core values are, and what legacy you want to leave. Put into words what your personal mission will be in retirement.

Do a situation analysis. Take an honest look at your strengths, weaknesses, threats, and opportunities. Howard suggested strengths might be more free time and the opportunity to travel. A weakness might be reduced finances. A threat could be some type of health problem. An opportunity could involve a new ministry at your church. Once the analysis is complete, you can begin to develop ways to address your weaknesses and threats and ways to take advantage of your strengths and opportunities.

Have a retirement vision. The first two steps provide knowledge to take to God in prayer and ask Him to give you a retirement vision of how best to continue your Christian calling (see Ephesians 4:1).

The idea is to envision the best future possible and plan to make that vision become concrete. Once the vision does come into focus, a retiree or a retired couple can plan steps to make the dream real and to reach goals within it. Howard suggested the vision would likely include categories such as spiritual life, family, physical, financial, personal growth, and heritage (for example, writing life stories to give to children and grandchildren).

Howard Foshee concluded, "So many times in retirement we keep thinking of leisure—what we can get out of life. We need to think about what we still can give to life. That's where real fulfillment comes." Howard and Zola Foshee have been practicing giving all their lives but especially in retirement.

Retirement continues to call for us to be good stewards of the time and blessings God gives us. Whether we approach retirement without a list of specifics or with a list and in a more systematic way, we are still accountable for working "while it is day." Since you're still reading in retirement, that means you're still writing the last chapter of life with all of its minichapters. So there is opportunity and hope to make retirement a climax and not an anticlimax of life. Or to put it another way, it's not too late to change the epitaph of your life and exchange your days for what has most value of all.

REFLECTIONS AND PROJECTIONS

- Before retirement, what did you exchange the days of your life for? Looking back, what gave you the most value for the investment of your life?
- The day before you retired, who were you? How did you identify yourself to others?
- Since retirement, what significant contributions have you made to anyone or anything?
- Looking at your retirement dreams against your retirement realities, what one pattern would you most like to change? How do you plan to go about it?
- If your epitaph depended only on your retirement life, how should it read?

RETIREMENT WORDS FROM THE WORD

John 9:4; Matthew 16:26; Ecclesiastes 3:11–13; James 2:26

PRAYER THOUGHTS

Father, thank You for letting me exchange the days of my life for Your blessings that have been greater than I deserved. Thank You for designing life with work and play and laughter and joy. Help me to balance life by choosing to live it fully, and help me to be a good steward of retirement. May I be worthy of hearing You pronounce upon my life, "Well done, thou good and faithful servant." Amen.

THE CHANGING NEST

Time will teach thee soon the truth,
There are no birds in last year's nest!

HENRY WADSWORTH LONGFELLOW,

It Is Not Always May

T he Bible often compares the home to a nest. Numbers
24:21 (KJV) reads, "Strong is thy dwellingplace, and thou
puttest thy nest in a rock." Proverbs 27:8 (KJV) says, "As a bird
that wandereth from her nest, so is a man that wandereth from
his place." Jesus noted that birds have nests, but He Himself
didn't have a place to lay His head (Matthew 8:20).

Poets have also compared the home to a nest. Longfellow
echoed what Cervantes had written much earlier, namely, "Never
look for birds of this year in the nests of the last" (*Don Quixote*).
In "The Marshes of Glynn," Sydney Lanier wrote:

As the marsh hen secretly builds on the water sod,
Behold I will build me a nest on the greatness of God.

In "Divine Songs," Isaac Watts observed:

Birds in their little nests agree;
And 'tis a shameful sight,
When Children of one family
Fall out, and chide, and fight.

I like the comparison of a home to a nest. However, it is worth recalling that a home without a family is just a house. So I'm writing both about the family and the house. The home is a nest that needs fresh consideration for each new season of life. And this need is especially true in the retirement season of life.

THE CYCLE OF LIFE

At the risk of being picky—but with a purpose—let me point out that Cervantes and Longfellow weren't completely right in saying that we ought not look for birds of this year in the nests of the last. I asked a bird expert if birds always build new nests each year or ever use their old ones. He said that birds do usually build new nests because of the winter deterioration of last year's nest and its unsuitability for the new year. However, he added that he had personally watched a robin add another lining of grass and twigs on an existing layer of a mud nest for two years in a row. He also said that older birds are more likely to build on an existing nest than younger birds are. Reference books reveal that the golden eagle builds a large nest, uses it from year to year, and increases its size until it sometimes reaches six feet in diameter. White-throated swifts and other birds may reuse the same nesting site for years.

Although humans are sometimes referred to as birds, they are not birds; nevertheless humans can learn from the comparison.

The *normal* cycle of life goes something like this for adult humans: meeting, courtship, mating, producing young, rearing young, emptying the nest, becoming a duo again, and becoming single again. It is because of this dynamic nature of the life cycle that I said the nest needs fresh consideration for each season of life. The nest may need to be new or to expand as the family expands. Then as the nest empties, it may need to be remodeled, adapted, or a new nest may be called for to match the changing size, needs, and wants of the family.

A LIFE CYCLE EXAMPLE

John Godwin and Dimple Aiken met, had a magnetic attraction to each other, courted, married on October 22, 1933, and mated in their early twenties. For their first west Texas home, they rented a small two-room apartment that had been servant quarters for the old Haley Hotel in Midland, Texas. The bathroom was next door in the hotel itself.

On February 20, 1937, I was in such a hurry to get started in life that I was born about 4:00 a.m. in that little servants' nest instead of in a hospital. The Godwin home had entered a new season of life. The nest needed to expand, and it did. Despite Depression era times, John and Dimple managed to move to a larger apartment; in time, they bought a small house shortly before Bill, another bird, appeared in the nest. Years later, after Marylyn, a longed-for daughter, was born, they bought a larger house to fit the needs of the growing family. Later, Paul, an adopted son, became the last bird to join the nest.

The whole story of John and Dimple Godwin and their family would be a book in itself, but for our purposes, we'll just focus on the changing nest. In time, I left for college and vacated a bedroom, a bathroom, and a place at the table. Next, my brother Bill left home, then my sister, Marylyn, and finally my brother Paul. The fledglings were gone, and John and Dimple had an empty nest. However, the nest was paid for, still suited them, and provided space for visiting children and grandchildren. So they kept it right on into retirement years.

After thirteen years of retirement, the duo became a solo again when John died and left Dimple widowed. From the very beginning, the nest had been changing, and the life cycle was almost complete. But not quite.

In this case, seventy-seven-year-old widowed Dimple was determined to keep on living independently in her own nest. Despite invitations we children issued for Mother to move in with one of us (over three hundred miles away) or move nearby in an apartment or assisted living facility, she refused for over eleven more years. Dimple was widowed and legally blind, but she had her own mind. She was able-bodied and made her own choices. She would say about her nest of almost fifty years, "I want to live in my own home until the Lord takes me to my heavenly home." She almost did that, but events in the last year of her life kept her from fully completing that wish. I'll tell you more about that later, but for now it's enough to see the scenario of one type of life cycle completed.

As the oldest child, I'm on top of the totem pole to complete the next generation's life cycle. And though I love the nest Phyllis and I occupy, I'm not as attached to it as Mother was to hers. But I do know it's best to look down the road and make choices for yourself before health or family or others force a choice upon you.

THE CHANGING FAMILY

What I spoke of as the *normal* cycle of life almost seems *abnormal* in the new millennium. The world has never been as connected or as fragmented as it is now. It's not only unwired but coming unwound. Although there is a World Wide Web for immediate communication and mind-boggling information, families often seem tangled in society's cobwebs.

In the midst of our society's choice explosion, families are often indecisive as they try to choose preferred alternatives from endless choices. We face extremes that may range from golden years of retirement to a kind of hell on earth. So focusing on the changing nest is more than a chapter to help fill up a book; it is a chapter to make a critical difference in retirement living. The challenge is to know alternatives, choose preferred alternatives, and follow up early with decisive actions.

I prefer to let others deal with the whole gamut of current family and social problems so that you and I can keep our focus on retirement. However, retirement doesn't take place in isolation from society, so it's important to look at the changing family in its relationship to retirement. To do that, it will be helpful to focus on these factors: (1) God's retirement design for the family; (2) what's actually happening in families today; and (3) alternatives retirees can choose from as the nest changes.

EMPTYING THE NEST

God's design for the family. Parenthood is forever. As long as parents and children live, they have a relationship and a responsibility to each other. Families have crises and should always be there for one another. *But the nest and retirement aren't forever.* After God had created woman, He said, "Therefore shall a man leave his father and his mother, and shall cleave unto his wife: and they shall be one flesh" (Genesis 2:24 KJV). God's plan for children to leave shows that He designed the nest to be emptied of its fledglings so they could become independent and have their own families and lives. When the parents push the fledglings out, it may be a traumatic experience for all of them (Isaiah 16:2). But independence—without alienation—is God's design, and, as a rule, it's best for both parents and children.

Further, the emptying of the nest is not intended to be a hard, calloused experienced but one of love. Children should always be welcomed back home, but after marriage or getting out on their own, they have a new home; the old home is no longer their home. It's a home for them to visit gladly but, ideally, no longer their home to live in.

The Bible pictures this: "As an eagle stirreth up her nest, fluttereth over her young, spreadeth abroad her wings, taketh them, beareth them on her wings: So the LORD alone did lead him" (Deuteronomy 32:11–12 KJV).

I once wrote a book titled *A Security Blanket Called Home* (Convention Press: Nashville, 1974). And in that book, I compared the emptying of the nest to the transition from winter to spring. When we think winter is over and the blanket is no longer needed, we take it off the bed and fold it up. But the cold returns, and we get the blanket out again for warmth. We may do this several times until spring really has come to stay. And children may need to return home more than once for a time, but the nest is not designed for them to occupy forever. Although there are exceptions, the rule is that children need to leave their birth home and establish their own home.

What happened in our family. Phyllis and I raised three sons and experienced the gladness of seeing them marry well but also the sadness of seeing them leave home. But all three have happy homes and are raising their own fledglings.

In the bird world, there are basically two kinds of baby birds: (1) the kind that quickly use their wings and are able to fly away on their own (the nidifugous); and (2) the kind that require longer nurturing and care before they're able to leave the nest (the nidicolous, which sounds like ridiculous). We had two sons who were nidifugous and one who was nidicolous. The sons left home and married at different ages and stages, but they emptied the nest. And any returns were only brief respites until they could strengthen their wings and fly on their own. They and their wives gave us eight grandchildren. The new families enrich our retirement lives immeasurably, and we visit each other's nests often.

When God's design for the family is carried out, retirees experience a new kind of freedom to enjoy retirement and be productive in it. This freedom doesn't justify selfishness or an indulgent retirement lifestyle; rather, it opens the door to enjoy God's blessings and to continue His calling in both continuing and new expressions.

What's happening in other families. Today many families are continuing the God-designed pattern. But that's not what's happening in multitudes of other families. The trend has been for boomers to marry later than their parents did, have children later, retire earlier, and often retire with children at home.

Divorce and remarriage have mushroomed and produced multiple families that are fragmented or interleaved in a variety of ways. Among all of this, millions of others are bypassing marriage altogether—whether they produce children or not.

Generation X-ers seem headed toward the same trends.

Many grown children are choosing a parasitic lifestyle that allows them to stay in the nest and sponge off their parents indefinitely. Often they pay no rent and spend all they make on themselves.

Choosing a preferred alternative. Parents have to choose whether they will let such an aberration from God's design continue on into their retirement years. I know a single parent whose bird wouldn't leave the nest. Finally, she told him, "The lease is up on this apartment. I'm renting another apartment that has only one bedroom and one key. You're going to have to get a place of your own." Hard-heartedness? No, just loving discipline to cause a fledgling to get a life of his own.

Parents facing retirement in the default mode of supporting parasitic children need to make a firm decision: Is this how they want to live their retirement life, or will they choose another kind of life? What's best for the retirement nest? Well, love should be foundational in making choices. Other factors include family spirit, flexibility, a sense of humor, economics, and serious retirement planning.

Further, in thinking about choices, it's wise to avoid either-or thinking. There may be a dozen or more alternative ways to deal with the changing nest at retirement. Both in the matter of emptying the nest and other choices, it's good to look at all possible alternatives, prioritize them, and choose the best one for each stage of retirement. Sometimes this approach calls for plans A, B, C, D, and so on; at different stages of retirement, second choices may have to take the place of first choices. I'll talk more about this when we get to the next chapter on "The Sandwich Generation." But for now let's think about the retirement nest apart from the fledglings.

A Nest for Each Season

Keeping the old nest. Suppose you retire in good health with adequate income and like where you live. Then why should you change anything about the nest you like and are comfortable in? Perhaps there is no reason to change anything in your home for the first season of retirement.

Nevertheless, retirement is an occasion for considering your wants, needs, and best decisions about housing. Consider the size, age, and maintenance requirements for your current home. Consider the location of your home. Is it in the neighborhood you want to keep on living in? Is it close enough to medical facilities, shopping centers, your church, other family members, and other places you plan to go to regularly? Do you feel safe? Given a choice, is your nest where you want it to be and what you want it to be in retirement? If so, stay there. If not, explore options for downsizing, rightsizing, or relocating.

Trying out a new nest. A lot of retirees change their nests rather quickly when they retire. Then many of them settle in their new digs only to regret that they've given up where they were and come to where they are. This unhappiness especially occurs when mates haven't come to a happy agreement about their retirement location, the kind of home they need, and the lifestyle they plan to share.

I've known folks to retire from Hawaii to Florida and then on to other locations without finding satisfaction anywhere. I've known others to relocate from a place of extreme seasons of cold or heat for a uniform climate and then be sorry for that choice. *Utopia* literally means "nowhere." Some places are better to live than others, but retirees have to bring a good deal of happiness with them because a location won't provide everything they're looking for.

Many retirees have moved from a big old house to a condo and suffered claustrophobia. If possible, it's good to try out a different nest and its location with the option of returning to the old one for a period of time. That approach can save a lot of heartache, a lot of money, and a lot of unnecessary moving around.

ADAPTING THE NEST

Whether retirees remain in their old nest or move to a new one, changing seasons usually call for adapting the nest for best retirement living. Moving some walls and remodeling may provide a home office, a shop, a sewing room, or separate areas for TV-watching and reading. This relatively simple effort can keep mates from colliding physically and emotionally as they feel the need for solitude in the midst of so much retirement togetherness. In other words, match the form of the house to the retirement functions and needs that go on there.

With rare exceptions, aging calls for some changes in the physical surroundings at home. If there are stairs, it might be wise to invest in a chair device to ride up and down the stairs, and it might be helpful to move bedrooms or other most-used rooms to the first floor. Elder eyes usually require considerably more light than younger eyes do for reading and good seeing. Even those facing retinopathy or other visual impairments can profit by well-focused lighting and plenty of it. (The American Association of Retired Persons—AARP—has excellent help in this area: http://www.aarp.org.)

When Mother was still a sprightly octogenarian in her own nest, she tripped on a throw rug and crashed to the floor. That fall broke her pelvis. While she was recovering in a rehab hospital, she had another fall that dislocated her shoulder. At that time, her family doctor said that a few years ago such accidents would have been the kiss of death for a woman in her eighties.

But not long after all the pain, hardship, and rehab treatments, Mother was back at home living independently—for the most part. However, the rehab professionals visited the home with Mother and suggested adaptations to keep further accidents from happening.

My sister saw to it that the rehab specialist's counsel was followed up on. Throw rugs were removed, and carpet edges got smoothed coverings over them. A furniture obstacle in a hallway was removed. New handgrips were placed appropriately at entrance doors and in the bathroom. Mother didn't like some of the other suggestions, so she refused to take them. Mother was still living independently and in charge, but her nest required some adaptation for a new stage of retirement life.

When the Old Nest Won't Do

More senior citizens than most of us are aware are able to live in their old nest until they die. They realize the dream that Job once stated: "Then I said, I shall die in my nest, and I shall multiply my days as the sand" (Job 29:18 KJV). And that's a great way to live out life. But we aren't always able to live in the old nest until God calls us to our new one (John 14:2–3). Long-term care insurance has helped make this dream possible for a lot of seniors, and Phyllis and I have bought some of it.

But retirees would do well to consider ahead of time what their second and later preferences would be if their nest had to change. Paul Tournier wrote, "At every stage in our lives it is important that our dwelling should suit the sort of life we live in it" (*Learn to Grow Old*).

One part of growing older often involves getting so much advice from one's children. Ideally, the parent and children should agree on what kind of dwelling best suits the retiree's life. But as long as the parent is of sound mind and is physically able, the decision of where to live still resides with the parent. Of course, we retirees ought not be unkind when our children express what they think is best for us even though it may not be what we want.

We ought not be stubborn beyond reason. We ought to be open to reevaluating what we want for ourselves, what is best for us, and what is best for us in light of our children and their desire to be our caregivers.

Depending on the circumstances, retirees may choose from several options: (1) a different but more suitable house, condo, or apartment for continued independent living; (2) home-sharing with family or someone of similar needs but retaining a good degree of privacy; (3) assisted living, with just as much or little help as needed with meals, transportation, amenities, and medical care; or (4) more complete total care of high quality. Personal choice, dignity, and quality of life are precious parts of personhood that call for full sensitivity and consideration by everyone.

When Dad was seventy-eight, he died the week after Thanksgiving. During that last Thanksgiving week, he and Mother had journeyed through Texas and Tennessee and visited all of their children, grandchildren, and great-grandchildren. When they got back home and settled in, Dad got the flu and died suddenly one morning. Sometime later, after the shock and grief were less, Mother began to say with thanksgiving, "Your daddy wasn't cut out for a nursing home." In other words, she was glad he hadn't had to leave the old nest before he died. Over the next several years, I realized Mother's statement about Dad really expressed her own feeling that she wasn't cut out for a nursing home (her all-inclusive term for anything but the home she was living in).

I don't suppose any of us are cut out for a nursing home; but if we can't have what we are cut out for, it's a good idea to have made our own best choices ahead of time. Retirement is a time for active decision-making, not for passive resignation. Your choices are yours to make.

Wherever our nest is, we can rest assured that God's eye is still on the sparrow. He provides for us now, and what He is preparing for us is better than any nest we've ever occupied on earth.

REFLECTIONS AND PROJECTIONS

- How did you feel about leaving home to establish your own home? How do you think your parents felt?
- How well have you planned for the changing nest of retirement?
- If your nest isn't empty, would you like for it to be? What plans do you have to nudge the fledglings toward independence?
- Describe your priority housing and location choice for the next ten years of retirement. Describe your second choice. God willing, what planning and decision-making do you need to do now to create the home you hope to live in for the next ten years?
- If you were no longer able to live independently, what would be your first choice? Second choice? Third choice? Share those choices with family and friends.

RETIREMENT WORDS FROM THE WORD

Luke 12:6; Luke 14:28; 2 Corinthians 3:5; Matthew 6:34; 2 Corinthians 5:1; John 14:2

PRAYER THOUGHTS

Father, help us to have the wisdom and courage to enable our children to empty the nest. May we look to You for insight and direction to choose our retirement location and housing. And may we turn any anxieties over to You with the confidence that You care for us and will provide for us. Amen.

CHAPTER TWELVE

THE SANDWICH GENERATION

*At every moment,
no matter what the accumulated ruins may be,
there is a plan of God to be found.*

PAUL TOURNIER

This chapter builds on the last chapter, which was about the changing family and retirement. However, this chapter's development is not nearly as neat as the last one. That's because the *Sandwich Generation* focuses on untidy circumstances that challenge retirees and their family members. Besides moving beyond the last chapter, I'm also repeating or emphasizing in different words points that are too important to mention only once.

Each developmental stage of life—each passage or hurdle—has its own job description. But when family members can no longer completely fulfill the part of life's job that calls for independent living, someone has to help them. And that someone is usually an adult child, a parent, a grandparent—or any combination of these three plus others.

Regardless of whether a retiree is a caregiver in the Sandwich Generation or a care-receiver, this matter is a part of retirement that calls for active love, wisdom, creativity, endurance, and hope. Since caregiving and care-receiving almost always become a part of retirement, we will do well to take a look at the *sandwich* and the *sandwiched*.

WHERE *SANDWICH* CAME FROM

We got the word *sandwich* from John Montagu, who was the fourth Earl of Sandwich (a town on the River Stour in Kent, England). One of Montagu's lesser vices was gambling for twenty-four hours or more at a time. When he had to choose either to stay at the gambling table or leave to eat, he wasn't satisfied with the either-or choice. So he made it a practice to get someone to bring him a slice of beef between two pieces of bread—and what we know as a sandwich was named after John Montagu in 1762. Later, "to sandwich" something came to mean to squeeze it in.

WHERE *SANDWICH GENERATION* CAME FROM

Dorothy Miller coined the term *Sandwich Generation* in 1981, and it has become a common term to describe adults who are sandwiched in by having to provide for their own parents and their own children—not to mention provision for grandparents and grandchildren.

Technically, a Sandwich Generationer is someone who has one or more aging parents who require help and at least one child at home. Typically, members of the Sandwich Generation are middle-aged and primarily women. However, the sandwich itself varies widely both in makeup and in ages of those involved. So for our retirement purposes, it seems most helpful to consider the context of the Sandwich Generation itself rather than focus on ages and gender.

In the early twentieth century, most people lost their parents before they themselves reached twenty-five years of age. In the early twenty-first century, there's a good chance that one or both parents of the new retiree are still living. The average life expectancy today is over seventy-five and going up. We now have our first whole generation of people living into their eighties and nineties and edging toward one hundred.

At the same time, couples have been marrying later than their parents did and having children later. For example, in the last generation or so, first-time births among women over forty increased by more than 50 percent. With the trend toward marrying later and having children later, more parents are retiring, semiretiring, or wanting to retire while their children are still living with them at home.

These factors have led to a Sandwich Generation of middle-agers who have caregiving responsibilities to both the younger generation and the older generation in their family. According to the U.S. Administration on Aging, more than one in four households nationwide are involved in caring for a relative or other loved one in need. Some 30 percent of caregivers are caring for two or more people, and over 60 percent of these caregivers are holding other jobs at the same time.

Households with at least one caregiver present have tripled since about 1990. Those receiving care may not live under the same roofs with their caregivers. In fact, geographical distance between the caregiver and the one requiring care is often part of what squeezes caregivers of the Sandwich Generation. In my sister's situation, she was the primary caregiver both for her own children and then for Mother, who lived over three hundred miles away. My sister lovingly bore this squeeze for many years.

CARING FOR THE CRUST

Elderly parents who can no longer manage life's responsibilities independently might be looked upon as the *crust*—the end of the loaf. The Sandwich Generation is responsible for its parents (see Mark 7:9–13). Those parents provided the first nest but can no longer maintain that independent nest without help. The parent-child fact does not change, but the respective roles change. The child still loves and honors the declining parents, but the functions change. In that sense, there is often a reversal of roles. All that our parents did for us when we were children is what we may now need to do for them. We may have to parent our parents while we're still parenting our own children.

This picture is not as bleak as it might seem at first, and I'll tell you why later. But for now, it's important to consider this factor in your own retirement plans and how it relates to your intergenerational family.

THE CLUB SANDWICH GENERATION

To complicate matters, the Sandwich Generation may find itself becoming a Club Sandwich Generation. The term *Club Sandwich Generation* came to me when I realized that another layer is increasingly being added to the basic sandwich. This trend especially affects retirees.

Let me explain. I know a retired couple who have one parent living with them. A divorced daughter came back home and brought a daughter with her. So members of four generations are living in that one house. In a Club Sandwich Situation, there are multiple slices of bread and more squeezing than in a simple sandwich.

Eight in ten adults over fifty are grandparents and spend over fifteen billion dollars a year on grandchildren for gifts alone. Many baby boomers and other grandparents are still raising children of their own while becoming primary or secondary caregivers for grandchildren. Instead of being footloose and fancy-free at retirement age, they're still buying kids' essentials such as clothing and diapers.

I first became aware of this challenge several years ago when I was leading a conference that focused partly on the empty nest and possible traumas related to it. A grandparent-looking-fellow in the audience raised his hand. When I acknowledged him, he said, "We didn't have any problem with the empty nest. In fact, we were elated when it became empty. Our problem was what to do with the empty nest refeathered." He explained that some of his grown children had returned home to live. That development obviously was not part of his retirement planning.

Sometimes these returnees are referred to as boomerang kids: They leave, but they tend to come back. More and more the boomerang kids are returning to their parents' nest with children of their own. Further, many of them come back to live as parasites. They contribute little or nothing; they take up space, eat up food, use utilities; they drain money, energy, and emotions. This situation is more common than you might expect.

More than four million U.S. children under eighteen live in grandparent-headed households. And the number is increasing.

Further, about one-third of these children in grandparent-headed homes don't have a parent present. The parent may become the missing link, the missing generation.

Although circumstances vary greatly, here are some factors involved in grandparents having to raise their grandchildren: the failure of adult children to mature to personal independence, the increase of divorce, and the trend of many to mate but not marry or provide a home.

Whatever the cause, many fledglings return home, deposit their offspring to be the responsibility of the grandparents, and leave again to do their own thing. Or both the children and the grandchildren may return to stay for an indefinite period in the nest that was supposed to be emptied at this retiree stage of life.

And, as I said earlier, children may necessarily be parenting their own parents. Therefore many people at retirement age are called upon to hold together a Club Sandwich Generation of both the young and the old. They are caught in the squeeze of multiple responsibilities for their own children, their own parents, and maybe also for their children and grandchildren at the same time.

Further, Sandwich Generationers are responsible for their own well-being and enjoyment in the midst of intergenerational strain. They may well have to put their own retirement plans on hold.

It's possible that retirees may miss being part of the Sandwich Generation or the Club Sandwich Generation. Not everyone is squeezed by the intergenerational bread. But when—and if—this squeezing happens, retirees may rightly feel they've lost part of their freedom and retirement. However, instead of depression, pessimism, or lost hope, it would be good to consider best alternatives in light of the circumstances.

An Open-Faced Sandwich

Remember how *sandwich* came into being? John Montagu refused to accept either-or thinking and came up with another solution: the sandwich. Retirees also need to be alert, creative, and thoughtful to avoid the trap of either-or thinking about the matter of getting squeezed. An open-faced sandwich, a smorgasbord, or a banquet may be possibilities.

Either-or thinking. Consider some typical examples of either-or thinking that Sandwich Generationers face: (1) I have to decide to spend time and energy with either my children and mate or with my parents. Either way, I'll feel guilty. (2) I have to decide either to give up things I enjoy in life or keep them at the expense of neglecting parents or my children and mate. (3) I either have to miss sleep to care for everyone's needs or leave needs unmet. (4) Either I have to meet everyone's needs myself or they won't get met. (5) I have to either abandon my retirement plans or put them on hold. All of these choices involve either-or thinking. Sometimes it's true there are only two choices, but that's not usually the case.

Preferred alternatives. I spend a good bit of time on the Internet and get a lot of e-mail. The e-mail includes everything from funny stuff to serious stuff. Often some of the serious stuff that someone feels needs sharing will end this way: "You can either share this message [as you ought to] or delete it [and be guilty]."

This close-ended alternative is an effort to manipulate readers to do what someone else wants them to do or take a guilt trip. Personally, I refuse to wear false guilt that someone else tries to impose on me. On the other hand, when I read such a message, I usually take time to consider other alternatives than the ones proposed.

The parallel point for those caught in the Sandwich Generation is this: Avoid false guilt, but also consider better alternatives than those that might first seem to be the only other solution. You can do better than be resigned to bad circumstances.

There are a lot of ways Sandwich Generationers can get relief from their squeeze and even find joy in the midst of it. But first they have to break the habit of either-or thinking. They have to do the creative work of digging for alternatives and choose the preferred or best alternatives.

I can't solve your problems for you and your unique situation. However, I can share some personal experiences and also tell you some possibilities that specialists recommend as partial solutions.

My Family's Sandwich Generation

What I am writing to you is not philosophy and statistics without experience. So let me put flesh and blood on what this chapter is about.

My parents. My parents followed God's design and reared their children toward independence. Otherwise, they would have crippled our lives. We all left home at different ages and stages. I left early and married early. During years of expensive schooling, I needed to return to my parents' home for a couple of summers, along with my wife and sons, so I could work and make money for more schooling.

Dad and Mother welcomed us home for those summers. Later, Dad and Mother provided home and care for my maternal grandmother and an adopted son. In their fifties they volunteered to become a Sandwich Generation out of great love and concern for others.

Our three sons. When our own three sons were grown and gone, we frankly enjoyed the empty nest. Then a son who was still single got into a financial bind and asked, "Dad, what do you think about me moving back home for a while?" I was not an unloving father who refused to do what my own dad had done for me. But because of this son's particular circumstances and developmental needs, I answered, "Let's consider another alternative."

As I saw it, this son was at a critical developmental stage in becoming independent or missing the timely chance for that growth. The bind was financial and not emotional. So I helped him face up to the fact that he needed to make some mature choices about how to spend his money and deal with priorities in paying off bills.

Further, he had looked at going back to a minimum-wage job because he didn't know what career he really wanted to pursue. I knew the supervisor in our corporate mail department, who specialized in helping boys become men. I managed to get him and my son together, and they became best friends.

This story ends positively. Tough love at the time paid off in a special way. Later, in his maturity and wisdom, he reflected on that time in life and rewarded me by writing: "Dad, love isn't always saying yes."

This son was at a critical stage of learning to fly on his own or not learning to fly at all. He learned to fly—and better than I ever dreamed.

Another of our sons, who was married and had children of his own, got caught in downsizing in another state and wound up without a job. When he asked about returning home and bringing his family with him until he got past this crisis, Phyllis and I were glad to say yes. The squeeze lasted only about four months. Then that son and his wife were able to fly on their own and later soar higher than we parents ever had.

Phyllis's mother. While our boys still lived with us in our Tennessee home, we got a call from Phyllis's mother, who lived in Texas. Though she had lived alone and worked outside the home for years, her voice trembled with anxiety as she explained she could no longer do that. She asked if she could come live with us. We didn't know what her problem was, but we gladly and quickly said yes. Phyllis went to Midland and helped her mother move to Tennessee.

Later, Vanderbilt doctors diagnosed Phyllis's mother as having Alzheimer's disease, which was new to our vocabulary at the time. The doctors were right in their diagnosis. And what began as a squeeze became a crush—primarily for dear Phyllis with all her family roles and her mother's dementia. Later, the doctors concluded twenty-four-hour care was absolutely necessary for both the safety and health of Phyllis's mother.

With anguished hearts, we and Phyllis's brother put their mother in the best nearby health-care facility available. For over ten years, Phyllis faithfully and lovingly visited her mother until a merciful death came. Grief was almost used up over the ten years, but still there was sadness mingled with a new gladness about the thought of reunion in heaven—where the new book will be far better than the old one for all believers.

Parents and siblings. Dad retired at age sixty-five, and he and Mother began thirteen years of good retirement together. At first they really didn't need much help and just enjoyed continuing to be family with all of us through phone calls, letters, and visits. Then Dad's vision deteriorated, and he had to quit driving. Dad had been a truck driver all his life and had continued some trucking in retirement. So the loss of his vision was especially grievous to him. And when he had to surrender his driver's license, my sister said big tears rolled down his cheeks.

But Mother was still able to drive, so Dad and Mother kept on going wherever they wanted to without needing much help. My sister, Marylyn, lived nearby at the time and was a caregiver when any help was needed. Marylyn, her husband, and family made a career move to the Dallas area. Then Dad died suddenly in good health at age seventy-eight.

Mother was left alone but with a deteriorating memory and diminishing sight that soon left her unable to drive. Both Marylyn and my brother Bill now lived over three hundred miles away. Phyllis and I lived a thousand miles away. Mother was seventy-seven and began to need help with the house and other things, so we siblings talked among ourselves.

We felt Mother should come to live with one of us or at least in the same city with one of us. But Mother was not brain-dead or wimpy. After vitamin B-12 shots and living alone for a while, her memory surprisingly got much better. She wouldn't hear of moving from her beloved Midland, Texas, where she had lived for more than fifty years.

I would preach her a one-on-one sermon about how the Bible taught that the eldest son was to take care of the mother. After she listened quietly, she would then get close to my face with her piercing blue eyes and preach me a sermon about how God had always taken care of her and always would and that it was a sin to worry. I remember on one such occasion that I told my little mother, "I'm the strongest one in our family, but you're stronger than I am." So with fierce independence and a mind of her own, Mother stubbornly chose to keep on living alone.

Although Marylyn had really been the primary caregiver for both Dad and Mother, she wasn't especially squeezed when she lived near them. But after Dad's death, Marylyn's primary caregiving role intensified. She had power of attorney over Mother's financial and medical affairs and devoted great attention to a long-distance support system for Mother when she herself couldn't be there.

Marylyn's fine husband and businessman, Dave, helped her manage Mother's financial affairs. Marylyn increasingly became a Sandwich Generationer, and she was squeezed. She was already stretched with her own husband, daughter and son, church and ministry, and personal needs. But with her supportive family and with strong love, this daughter became the great enabler for Mother to keep on living at least semi-independently with quality life.

After Dad died, Mother had a lot of pain to deal with over the next dozen years: She had an ulcer, underwent one major surgery for a tumor, broke a wrist, broke her pelvis, and dislocated her shoulder. In her last year of life, she fell twice and had to have two hip replacements, and she also began to experience increasing memory failure.

Still, for most of eleven years after Dad died, Mother had continued to go to church, enjoy a social life, and make contributions to almost everyone who pled their case for contributions. On rare occasions when no one came by to take Mother to church, despite her blindness, she would still manage somehow to get an operator on the line and call a taxi to take her to church. And someone would take her home.

Mother lived in Midland and belonged to the same church for sixty-seven years. She lived in the same house for almost fifty years. As a widow, she went to bed when she wanted to, got up when she wanted to, ate what she wanted, and pretty much did as she pleased. Her only real complaint was to say, "I'm healthy and have all the time in the world to help people, but I can't see to do a blooming thing."

My brother Bill and I and others did what we could; but with Marylyn's special daughter-mother relationship, she was the one who bore the brunt of almost constant caregiving. But finally when mother's dementia became bad enough to interfere with daily functioning, Marylyn did call on her brothers to help get Mother to the Baylor Geriatric Clinic.

At Baylor they diagnosed Mother as having a stage of Alzheimer's. Then the woman gerontologist lovingly took both of Mother's hands in her hands and gently told her she needed to live near Baylor and her daughter to get essential treatment. Dr. Nyack then asked Mother, "Is that all right?"

With both recognition and resignation, Mother quietly responded, "Well, I don't guess I have any other choice." So we moved her to an assisted living facility in the Dallas area.

It was after the move from Midland during Mother's last year that she experienced her two hip breaks and other problems. Even in that last year, though, she showed strong character and a thriving Christian witness in both assisted living and in a rehab home she lived in.

Mother died quietly one night—not quite having lasted in her own home until time for her heavenly home. Marylyn was with her. Later, all the staff in those caregiving places wrote personal notes with anecdotes about Mother and her time with them and about her Christian testimony.

I had wondered why God had left Mother on earth for that last year. But then I realized He had taken her on that side trip to be a witness once more before calling her home.

We had grieved a lot over Mother's deteriorating condition, but we had more gratitude than grief when God called her home on August 4, 2003, just two days before her eighty-ninth birthday. Her Midland funeral was a celebration fit for a saint—a feisty saint, and that she was.

Becoming the Crust

We Sandwich Generationers feel we're getting a peek at our own future as we watch our elderly parents. That peek may fill us with anxiety, dread, or possibly with conviction and peace. No matter where we are in the sandwich, we'll one day become the crust—the end of the loaf.

While we retirees are being Sandwich Generationers or emerging from that squeeze, we have the opportunity to decide how we want life to be when we become the crust. Mates can talk to God and between themselves to anticipate preferred alternatives for this stage of life.

Although first choices may have to yield to second or third choices, it's a good idea to plan how you would most like to continue to live life and be treated in dying. And it's good to share those thoughts with your children, who likely will become the next Sandwich Generation.

Mates do each other a favor if they anticipate and help prepare for the time when the duo will become a solo. More than 80 percent of those widowed in the U.S. are women, so it's likely the husband will die first. But he may not. Either way, husband and wife will do well to work as a team and prepare the smoothest way possible for the one who is widowed.

Joys for Sandwich Generationers

Rich rewards often come as serendipities when a family is

sandwiched together by circumstances. Children get to look through their parents' eyes in a different way and tend to discover more of their heritage. Parents who were lonely after their children left home now find themselves in renewed relationships and closer contacts. Grandchildren and grandparents separated by miles are brought together more often. And when all the sandwich is under one roof, laughter and humor may be brighter than the stereotypical gray tones associated with aging.

We can learn more about each other and more about life. Only in the last couple of years did I learn that Mother kept a diary most of her life. And she let me read in her diaries as much as I wanted. I read her happy entry for the day I was born. Her diaries were the only personal effects I asked for and received when she had to move from Midland. I read her recorded experiences joyfully and poignantly and began to transcribe them for family and posterity. My brother Bill started taking one year at a time of the e-mailed diaries and read them aloud to Mother when he visited. She said it was like living those years over again. What a blessing for all of us!

Another precious time during Mother's last years was to see her in the midst of her grandchildren and great-grandchildren. No one can adequately put into words what occurs when a grandmother magnetizes the heart of her youngest grandchild and they share a moment that locks itself into eternity. I've witnessed that, but I don't know how to put it on paper or into words. It came late but stays always.

The sandwich won't last forever; so despite the pressure, learn to find joy and pleasure in it. Or if that's hoping for too much, learn to compensate by getting help from others and making helpful trade-offs as you continue to express loving care.

Productive Retirement

Although no two retirements are exactly the same in every way, there are predictable elements that tend to be a part of most retirements. I heard the late Elton Trueblood say, "Don't retire from everything at once; rather, retire gradually from what you want to and have to." He also said that he was surprised when people would discover all he was doing and then comment, "Well, you're not really retired."

Elton found himself being productive in one way or another until he died in his midnineties. And he remained productive despite the grief of his first wife's death and his later caregiving for his second wife until she died. As he aged and faced health problems, he retreated from his pattern of traveling worldwide to teach others who would come to him. And he welcomed numerous people to his own home and campus for the mentoring he still loved to do. In various ways, he was sandwiched by family, health, and aging itself, but he remained productive.

Looking at predictable slices of retirement life, most all of us will find ourselves being squeezed by caring for a child, a parent, or a mate; often the squeezing will be from more than one direction. But every stage of retirement life can be productive in some way unless we give up and give in to the hard things that press and stress us. In fact—like the rest of life—we will not be productive if we wait until everything gets just right. Things seldom get just right, and if they do, they don't stay that way very long.

Thinking particularly about the Sandwich Generation, how can retirees avoid putting life on hold and decide to make the most of each stage of retirement?

Don't let temporary circumstances become permanent. While loving and caring for family members in crisis, refuse to let parasitic family members attach themselves to you. Exercise wisdom and tough love to help children become independent. Care for dependent parents in a way that doesn't enslave you or cause you to lose your own independence. And don't look at the present as if it were the rest of your life or retirement.

Determine to be productive despite circumstances. For example, keep your identity and sanity by planning at least one personal activity outside caregiving that you look forward to each week. Reduce optional negative drains on your life and time, and selectively keep on doing what seems most productive. Being sandwiched is something you can endure and change in time, but in the midst of the squeeze, the challenge is to find rays of sunshine and ways to remain both happy and productive. Give up false guilt and unhealthy resentment to enjoy yourself for a time.

Get help for what crushes you. The Bible specifically commands us to bear our own burdens but also to bear one another's burdens (Galatians 6:2, 5). This is not a contradiction; rather, it is a recognition that individuals have burdens to bear alone but require help for others. We can carry a stone but not a boulder. There is no virtue in wearing a martyr complex instead of asking for help. Where there are adult siblings, it is wrong for one to be the Lone Ranger in caregiving even if one bears a disproportionate amount of the load. Family members have no excuse for dumping caregiving on the closest sibling or family member. Where there are no siblings, it is wrong to deny yourself the help available through church, community, government, and creative ways to alternately share burdens.

Learn how to provide on-site care from a long distance. Family caregivers on-site or nearby and those at a distance need to have happy agreements that are good and fair. However, no family member may be nearby, so it's important to learn how to provide on-site care from a distance. The best source I've found for this kind of information comes from AARP (formerly known as the

American Association of Retired Persons, now known only by the initials). Anyone with computer access can get immediate information at http://www.aarp.org/life/caregiving. Or you can write to AARP at 601 E Street NW, Washington, DC, 20049. AARP also provides links to a world of specialized help for Sandwich Generation caregivers—retired or not.

Take frequent minisabbaticals. Regardless of how great and intense your caregiving responsibility is, give yourself a rest. You may not know how to do this, but there is a way. Just an hour, a day, a week or more away from being a Sandwich Generationer can be magic to the soul and recharge your life with energy and fresh perspective.

Give up regret. When retirement doesn't work out the way you thought it would or planned for it to, regret is a futile look backward. No one can say anything or do anything to change the past; it's gone. The present is here, and what you decide now will change the future. Whether you are widowed, have poor health, or have children and parents to care for, God has a plan for the present. And that plan calls for hope rather than regret, gratitude rather than grief, and joy instead of gloom.

Plan ahead. When you become the crust, or care-receiver, have your plans and preferences made and known. That preparation is your best assurance for continuing to choose the kind of retirement life you want to live. Further, the preparation will be a help to those who love you and care for you.

Regardless of the circumstances, remember that God has a plan for each moment of life; He has already planned for what we can't anticipate. So it is not a cliché or a platitude to counsel all of the Sandwich Generation to make prayer a priority for this special need in life.

REFLECTIONS AND PROJECTIONS

- If your grandparents or parents were ever Sandwich Generationers, how did they handle it? What would you have done differently?
- If your grandparents or parents retired, reflect on the stages of their retirement or semiretirement. What was most satisfying for them? Most frustrating?
- If you are caught in the middle as a retiree Sandwich-Generationer, identify at least two ways from reading this chapter that might offer some relief from your squeeze. Or come up with two ways of your own.
- If you don't see any solution to what is pressing on you right now, take at least one immediate step to get help from a family member, friend, counselor, or major resource such as AARP.

RETIREMENT WORDS FROM THE WORD

Exodus 20:12; Mark 7:11–13; Galatians 6:2, 5; 1 Peter 5:7; Philippians 4:13

PRAYER THOUGHTS

Father, help us to lovingly nourish our children and cherish our parents with honor and care. Help us to endure the pressures that squeeze our spirits and to rejoice and be glad in each day You give us. We pray for wisdom and courage to make right decisions that will blend caregiving and retirement joy. Amen.

Chapter Thirteen

Retirement with Attitude

*Attitude is the key to success or failure
in almost any of life's endeavors.*

Carolyn Warner

I t was recreation time in a Georgia resort at a publishers meeting I attended. For tennis we just paired up with whoever was available. My partner for the day was Tom Torbet of Appalachia, Inc. We had never played tennis together and got way behind in our match. During a pause, Tom came to me with a grin that barely covered his attitude of chagrin as we faced what looked like certain defeat. He asked, "Johnnie, do you want to forfeit, or do you want to lose graciously?" Either-or thinking never was my cup of tea and certainly not in that case. So I replied, "I want to win." Tom kind of flinched, stepped back, and got a new look in his eye. We played every point as hard as we could, and we won. Attitude made the difference, and it usually does—especially in retirement.

The Evolution of Attitude

About AD 1700, the word *attitude* came into English from French, Italian, and Latin to express manner of feeling, thinking, posture, fitness, and disposition. Sometimes early English spelled *attitude* as *aptitude*, which came from the Latin spelling and originally meant likelihood or disposition. So *attitude* and *aptitude* were closely related from the beginning. In other words, we're apt to do what our attitude is. And the habitual attitudes we have in retirement will largely determine our retirement enjoyment and success—or our misery and defeat. You see, retirement isn't automatically life's best chapter. That's a choice to make.

In recent years the word *attitude* has taken on some relatively new meanings. One newer meaning of *attitude* is to have an assertive or arrogant state of mind, a testy or uncooperative disposition. Not long ago, I heard this usage when a customer was kidding a sales clerk and couldn't get the best of her. He facetiously said, "That's just what we need: a sales clerk with an attitude."

Another more recent shade of meaning for *attitude* is that of having the right stance in a spirited manner. I'll illustrate that for you. Awhile back I was on a dude ranch near Scottsdale, Arizona, with a bunch of other city dudes who usually wore suits. We were gathered outside with a mix of cowboys and cowgirls for a western cookout and recreation.

One of the planned activities was for experts to teach us how to line dance. Being a Baptist preacher, I didn't even know how to square dance, but Phyllis pushed me into trying to learn how to line dance. I nervously gave it a timid but polite try.

One of the expert line-dance instructors noticed that I had

two left feet and that I was kind of backward about making the effort needed. She told me, "You're going to have to get an attitude if you want to learn how to line dance right." She meant I needed to let my hair down, get with the program, strut my stuff, and not worry about what anyone thought if I were to get any enjoyment out of the activity. She meant that my attitude needed to be spirited, not passive. Well, I've still got two left feet, but boy did I ever have fun when my attitude changed. And that's what this chapter on "Retirement with Attitude" is about.

DON'T BE CRUSTY

In the preceding chapter, you'll remember I talked about the Sandwich Generation and about retirees eventually becoming the crust—the end of the loaf. If we live long enough, that's going to happen; but that's no excuse for becoming crusty in attitude.

Retirees may have lived a lifetime of statesmanship and good etiquette that caused them to disguise many of their real attitudes. That's part of the politeness of life and isn't hypocrisy. It's often just good sense and good business to curb the expression of attitudes that won't help and are likely to hinder. But many folks seem to feel that retirement and old age provide a license for being frank and candid—which often translates into brutally frank and cuttingly candid. No one likes being around a person with an acrid attitude and speech that cuts like acid.

So it's good to sort out our attitudes and decide which ones we'll live retirement by. Maybe it would be helpful to click through some negative attitudes we need to get rid of or be especially cautious about in retirement. Paul Tournier knew what he was talking about when he wrote, "A person's characteristics tend to become more accentuated as his life goes on." And he added, "Therefore, if one's old age is to be happy, there must be a change of attitude" (*Learn to Grow Old*).

BYPASS SELF-PITY

Some retirees adopt an attitude of self-pity and throw regular pity parties for themselves. This tends to happen when the children grow up, empty the nest, move off, and have a life of their own. The children are in the midst of busy careers, raising their own kids, and doing things with their immediate family. Retirees' children may not call, write, or visit often enough to suit their retired parents. In our solitude, we may begin to feel and act pitiful. And when we do have contact with our children, we may lay a false guilt trip on them and spoil the contact. Retirees need to recognize and avoid such destructive and self-defeating attitudes.

Whiny, wimpy retirees face the challenge of getting outside themselves and helping others. It's hard to feel self-pity when you're helping those who are far worse off than you are.

Besides all that, there is the possibility that older parents may live longer if they don't devote themselves only to their own children. I got this inference from a German study of male senior citizens. Those male senior citizens whose lives revolved around the success or social support of their children tended to die about four years sooner than those who had friends and interests reaching beyond their children (*Men's Health*, Nov. 1999).

Now I don't know about women parents and any similar relationship to their mortality. But either way, it's generally accepted that it's emotionally healthy to have broader friendships than just family and to have intergenerational friendships. Someone has said that we need old friends to grow old with and new friends to keep us young. And those same friends may unknowingly help us bypass self-pity.

RETREAT FROM RESENTMENT

Few people reach retirement age without having been slighted, insulted, mistreated, or injured in some way that could result in resentment. On rare occasions, this attitude of ill will and negative feelings sometimes gnaws its way back into my own life like a recurring ulcer. I hear a person's name, get some reminder of a hurtful experience, or just find myself letting the devil replay a past resentment. But I know resentment can ruin a perfectly good time in my retirement, so I don't engage it for long but retreat from it to more positive attitudes.

Further, when I do become conscious of any creeping resentment, I don't treat the symptoms with emotional Rolaids; rather, I try to go back to the cause of resentment and root it out. That's easier said than done. But I've found help in adopting Lucille T. Wessmann's retirement counsel. She wrote, "My advice is this: If at all possible, don't cut your bridges to what you've done and where you've been."

I like to recall the treasure of my career years, enjoy remembering my colleagues, breathe a prayer of goodwill for anyone who wronged me or rubbed me the wrong way. And I wish the best for those who succeeded me. I haven't burned any bridges of relationships nor let resentment shut a door to return visits to those relationships—whether the visits are just in my mind or become real visits.

Your resentments are your own, but they'll own you and

your retirement if you entertain them for long. So it's a good idea to retreat from resentment.

LOOK AWAY FROM REGRET

Regret is a futile focus on an unchangeable past. Regret looks at some negative thing done or undone in the past and results in present pain and remorse. Retirement provides both time and occasion for regret. Family and friends may have died before we made peace with them or shared something in our heart. Arthur Hopkins said, "There is a wealth of unexpressed love in the world. It is one of the chief causes of sorrow evoked by death: what might have been said or done that never can be said or done." Despite this truth, regret won't help one bit.

In a similar way, regret won't help change any other area of life's past tenses. The talent or skill we didn't develop won't be developed by looking backward. The stock or real estate investment that would have made us rich or prosperous or bankrupted us is hindsight that won't help. No one can change the past except historians, and they mostly do it by accident, ignorance, or deceit.

Helen Keller pointed the better way and the better attitude. She said, "When one door of happiness closes, another opens, but often we look so long at the closed door that we do not see the one which has been opened for us." Or, more simply, she who was blind saw that we need to look away from regret and look forward to future possibilities.

GET OVER GRIEF

When a mate or other loved one dies, lingering grief can freeze or end the effective life of a survivor. Most of us have seen someone who has given in to unending grief. A child may die, and a parent may preserve everything of the child's except the life of the parent. Though time goes on, the parent really doesn't go on but exists in a frozen past. When mates are close and one of them dies, the other may be grieved to death or fail to get over grief and start a new life.

Even though resurrection is a promise and a certainty, I would not minimize the need to grieve. Grief is a natural attitude of hurt to experience and then to be healed from. In the Bible, Naomi lost her husband and two sons to death. When she returned from Moab to Bethlehem, her grief was so great she changed her name from Naomi, "my pleasantness," to Mara, "bitterness" (Ruth 1:19–20).

Life's happiness seemingly was over for Naomi. But after Boaz married Ruth, she bore a son they named Obed. The Bible records a song of joy the women sang to Naomi about the birth of Obed: "He shall be to you a restorer of life and a nourisher of your old age; for your daughter-in-law who loves you, who is more to you than seven sons, has borne him" (Ruth 4:15 NRSV). "Then Naomi took the child and laid him in her bosom, and became his nurse" (Ruth 4:16 NRSV). Bitterness left, and pleasantness returned—full circle. In effect, Mara became Naomi again.

If statistics continue the present trend, most female retirees will become widows, and perhaps about 20 percent of male retirees will become widowers. It is important to grieve when that happens, but it is equally important to get over grief; for there may yet be a generation of joy and years more of productive living for the survivor.

DEFEAT DEPRESSION

Depression is an attitude of gloom, doom, and darkness. It's akin to grief, but there may or may not be an apparent reason for feeling so down and dismal. Besides obvious factors that plunge a person into depression, the medical community knows that a hormonal imbalance can be involved in depression. There are helpful medications for depression, and good counseling can often get at the causes and cures of depression.

Although I'm not a medical doctor or a psychologist, I'm acquainted with depression, and I know that it likes to accompany retirement. Sooner or later retirement usually offers occasion for depression. An uncle of mine lived until his early eighties and experienced a decline of health that pretty much reduced his enjoyable activities to eating and watching TV.

When I visited my uncle, he told me with anguish, "I used to be able to do everything; now I can't do anything." He didn't live long after that. When I spoke on a Sunday morning in a rehab hospital, I faced a legless man who was younger than my uncle but unable to do much more than my uncle had been able to do. Somehow, though, this man spoke up and gave thanks for blessings he had left rather than being depressed over what he had lost. Judith M. Knowlton got at the difference with this statement: "I discovered I always have choices, and sometimes it's only a choice of attitude." Choosing the right attitude is one of the best ways to defeat depression.

During years of schooling, I pushed myself day and night until my body rebelled and my spirit crashed in exhaustion and depression. For me, the sun wouldn't shine, and nothing anyone could say or do would remove my darkness or brighten my life.

As I shared in the chapter on "Body and. . ." my Christian

doctor told me I had a physical problem, not a faith problem. Over a summer with rest and the medication of a newly discovered antidepressant, I got up one day and discovered the sun was still shining. My family was well; the birds were singing; natured reflected God's artistry.

For the life of me, I couldn't figure out why I had been depressed, but I determined not to get that kind of depression again. And I taped a note to my shaving mirror that read, "Depression hurts and doesn't help. Smile!" It was a reminder to me and not just a gimmick, and I still quote that saying to myself. I've been depressed a bit from time to time since then but never like that dark night of the soul when I was a young man.

I've shared this with you simply to say I know something about depression, and I'm empathetic with those who fight it. It's best not to get depressed, but should you get depressed in retirement, use every resources possible to get rid of it.

I found help in Bible verses such as 1 Peter 5:7, in prayer, in soothing music, in rest, in hard physical labor, and in medication administered by a fine Christian doctor and counselor. I recommend those same resources to you. Willpower alone isn't enough to end the kind of depression I described, but I'm convinced it's important to recognize depression and to will an attitude of joy instead of gloom.

RECOGNIZE SYMPTOMS OF AGE RAGE

- Being easily bothered and exploding over little or nothing
- Thinking we're ugly or being sullen because we can't do what we want to or used to do

- Being churlish over relatively insignificant changes
- Having an inner attitude that's negative spirited rather than positive spirited

MOVE FROM THE NEGATIVE

There are other unhealthy attitudes we ought to avoid in retirement, but the ones we've looked at so far seem to have a special liking for retirement-age folks. Many others have recognized the importance of moving from the negative to the positive.

Julia Seton wrote, "We have no more right to put our discordant states of mind into the lives of those around us and rob them of their sunshine and brightness than we have to enter their houses and steal their silverware." Lydia M. Child said, "You find yourself refreshed by the presence of cheerful people. Why not make an honest effort to confer that pleasure on others? Half the battle is gained if you never allow yourself to say anything gloomy." Psychologist William James wrote, "The greatest discovery of my generation is that a human being can alter his life by altering his attitude."

ACCENTUATE THE POSITIVE

Most of us are well familiar with books and teachings on the power of positive thinking, but we may not have realized the power of negative thinking. While Christians know that self-help is not enough help, we also know that in Christ we have the power to be can-do people (Philippians 4:13). It is this undefeatable spirit that serves as the best foundation for positive retirement attitudes.

A positive attitude is largely a matter of choice. People in almost identical circumstances often have opposite attitudes. That's especially noticeable in retirees. Some have an attitude of gratitude about all they're still able to do, and they give thanks for all their blessings. They do this in spite of whatever they've had to give up and regardless of health problems. One living example of this kind of spirit is a new friend of mine named Harv, whom I met in Mother's last rehab hospital. He's relatively young but is there most of the time with severe multiple sclerosis. Yet he reads and can still underline positive passages in books I've shared with him. He's a Christian and has a radiant smile and a spirit that lifts me up.

People in desperate circumstances but with positive attitudes are those who choose to live their lives in a major key of hope rather than a dark, minor key of despair. I've observed that those who accentuate the positive are mostly those who live beyond themselves and focus on others rather than dwelling on themselves.

The cynic looks upon retirement as "the liberation of a captive butterfly just as its wings begin to crumble" (*The Cynic's Dictionary*). The positive realist doesn't deny a decline in health or abilities but chooses to focus on the liberation of retirement.

I don't apologize for repeating the counsel of my late Christian philosopher friend Elton Trueblood: "Don't retire from everything at once but gradually from each thing as you have to or want to." He modeled what he counseled until he died at ninety-four. He chose that attitude and lived it consistently even when his own sphere of activities shrank step-by-step and year by year.

In Mother's last year of life, I heard some of her most spontaneous and pure laughter. One aide told how she had been wheeling Mother down a hall in a wheelchair when Mother shouted, "Woo-woo! Watch out; here comes Dimple Godwin!" Mother had been to sorrow and back more times than I want to remember, but her visits to joy and laughter seemed frequent almost until death overcame her earthly life. She refused to give in to grief and despair over what she had lost. She continued to give thanks and say near the end, "Hasn't God blessed us with a wonderful life? We've got so much to be thankful for." Mother accentuated the positive.

AGE GRACEFULLY

For a long time, I've heard people talk about aging gracefully, and I suppose I've equated that with being placid, if not passive. Being passive never appealed to me. But at the heart of the word *grace* is a blend of love, kindness, and active goodwill. Given those blends of meaning, *grace* merits commendation as a retirement attitude.

Jesus more than anyone else lived life with an attitude of grace as well as providing saving grace for us. The apostle Paul was inspired to write, "Your attitude should be the same as that of Christ Jesus" (Philippians 2:5 NIV). Jesus' attitude was one of active grace determined to complete the will of the Father.

Grace is also kin to joy. And when people age gracefully, they have a gladness, a poise, and a dignity about them that is admirable. Over forty years ago, I was Grace Hardy's pastor, and she bore all the qualities of her name at about age fifty. I never saw Grace and husband Lee again after my seminary days—until about two years ago. Grace contacted us with the help of one of her daughters who searched on the Internet.

We've visited three times since then.

Grace still has those same qualities she's always had as she prepares to move into her nineties, and she e-mails us. Lee is in his nineties. He plays solitaire on the computer, and his humor is still dry and wonderful. People like Grace and Lee have attitudes that are admirable. They seem to know how to put adversity in perspective and not give in to it. They seem to hear and obey an eleventh commandment that says, "Thou shalt not whine."

Those with grace have a maturity about them that matches their retirement years. I read somewhere that growing older is inevitable, but growing up is optional. That's a simple way of saying what psychologists have taught us for years: Reaching maturity is a developmental task—a job—for each stage of life. Those who age gracefully are not childish retirees, but that doesn't mean they're wooden or lacking in fun.

DISCOVER WHAT REAL PATIENCE IS

When most people think of "the patience of Job," I suppose they still think Job was calm and imperturbable in the midst of his troubles. That wasn't true; he was anguished. "The patience of Job" refers to the endurance of Job. It was Job who said about God, "Though he slay me, yet will I trust in him" (Job 13:15 KJV). One of the key attitudes for retirees to choose and to hang on to is the kind of patience that endures hardship.

Winston Churchill spoke with passion about this kind of endurance in a speech to boys at Harrow School in England on October 29, 1941. He urged them, "Never, never, in nothing great or small, large or petty, never give in except to convictions of honor and good sense." The same counsel is vital for retirees if they're going to make life's last chapter with its minichapters the best of the book.

One retiree who had the attitude of not giving up fell and injured herself badly. After weeks in a rehab hospital and a setback while there, she was heard to say, "I feel like going home and just giving up." She almost lost the patience that endures, but she hung on and recovered from her injuries. She stayed in charge of her life and lived with grit and grace until she exchanged this life for the next one.

The more traditional understanding of patience as waiting without being perturbed is also important in retirement. Someone defined that kind of patience as "having something to do while you wait." I'm not very patient in this, but busying myself with something meaningful tends to help me while I wait.

One car manufacturer noted that the average person spends six months of his life in his car waiting for red lights to turn green. The point of the ad was to focus on the enjoyable surroundings within the car and the fine sound system that could even make waiting on a red light an enjoyable experience. I wasn't made for red lights, but fine sound over my Bose speaker system in the car does make the wait more pleasant.

Some of us retirees often find ourselves frustrated by delays and red tape we have little or no control over. Ever-changing insurance matters are just one example of confusion many of us deal with. It may seem that nothing happens quickly, easily, or on time anymore—although I'm not sure that was ever true in the past either. Anyway, having something meaningful to do while you wait is an important factor in retirement patience. Such an attitude and such an approach is a gift to the body, mind, and soul. Blood pressure, peace of mind, and heartsease all tend to be better with an attitude of patience. I'm working on it.

LIVE WITH HOPE

When number one son Mark married Pam, they were both working and able to buy a starter house not far from us. When we went over to see their house, Pam was proud to show us through it room by room. When we got to the guest bedroom, there were twin beds and a plaque over each bed. One plaque read *Faith*, and the other read *Love*.

Since I'm of a theological bent, I asked, "Where is *Hope*?"

Pam quipped, "They don't come in *Hope*; they just come in *Faith* and *Love*."

I smiled, but her answer stayed with me: They don't come in *Hope*.

I've found that a lot of people are asking where hope is, and many retirees seem to think that retirement doesn't come in *hope*. But I'm here to tell you that all of life—and especially retirement—can have hope.

Generally speaking, hope is a wish tinged with optimism. However, the New Testament shows that hope is not a wish but a certainty for those who know Christ as Lord and Savior. The apostle Paul stated this plainly in writing to those who had been hopelessly lost but became Christians with hope. He wrote, "At that time ye were without Christ. . .having no hope, and without God in the world: But now in Christ Jesus ye. . .are made nigh by the blood of Christ" (Ephesians 2:12–13 KJV).

Apart from the God-directed life, there is no reason for hope instead of emptiness in life (see Ecclesiastes 1:2). Paul wrote, "To whom God would make known what is the riches of the glory of this mystery. . .which is Christ in you, the hope of glory" (Colossians 1:27 KJV).

This Christian attitude of hope is rooted in eternity, gives power in the present, and guarantees that things will get better. You may remember than when I used to tell Phyllis things would get better and they didn't, she would add, "In heaven." The Christian lives with the hope that things will get better on earth; but if not, the Christian lives with the certainty of hope that things will be better in heaven—in fact, they'll be perfect.

Paul wrote, "According to my earnest expectation and my hope, that in nothing I shall be ashamed, but that with all boldness, as always, as now also Christ shall be magnified in my body, whether it be by life, or by death" (Philippians 1:20 KJV).

Paraphrasing and blending thoughts I've heard from others, such as the late Ed Lindaman, I've concluded this: *Hope is the music of the future; love is its melody; and faith is to dance to it.* Retirees can have hope regardless of the accumulated ruins in their lives and whatever their physical condition. But rather than speaking of a Pollyanna hope, I'm talking about an attitude that plays the sharp notes on the keyboard of life rather than the flat notes, and the basis for such hope is found in Christ.

Near the end of Hubert Humphrey's life, he recalled how his parents had lost their home and most of their possessions during the Great Depression of the 1930s. Looking back on the time and the rest of his life, Humphrey said, "In life it isn't what you've lost; it's what you've got left that counts. . . . It was only a question of time before things would get better. The important thing was who would be the survivors. Who had the will to hang on for a better day?"

Roy Z. Kemp said, "There is no better or more blessed bondage than to be a prisoner of hope." Although many of our earthly hopes are never fulfilled, the attitude of hope still serves its valuable purposes in our lives. It helps us endure rather than give up. It causes us to look for springtime while we're living through winter. When life threatens to go stale, hope brings freshness. And it is hope that helps us overcome life's griefs, hurts, and scars.

In fact, when hope grows around where we have been injured the most, it is exactly there that we become the strongest—like a log that will not split because it has grown around its injuries and is toughest at the very spot of its injury. I know because I've tried to split logs like the one I've described. A similar thing can happen in the lives of retirees who have hope.

Charlotte Barnard wrote:

I cannot sing the old songs,
Or dream those dreams again.

But with grander insight, Oliver Wendell Holmes challenged us:

Build the more stately mansions, O my soul,
As the swift seasons roll!
Leave thy low-vaulted past!

And I especially think retirees profit by having the kind of hope Bonnie Prudden wrote about. She said, "You can't turn the clock back, but you can wind it up again."

Father Keller, who founded The Christophers, wrote "Hope in Action":

Hope looks for the good in people instead of harping on the
worst.

Hope opens doors where despair closes them.
Hope discovers what can be done instead of grumbling
about what cannot.
Hope draws its power from a deep trust in God and the
basic goodness of mankind.
Hope "lights a candle" instead of "cursing the darkness."
Hope regards problems, small or large, as opportunities.
Hope cherishes no illusions, nor does it yield to cynicism.
Hope sets big goals and is not frustrated by repeated
difficulties or setbacks.
Hope pushes ahead when it would be easy to quit.
Hope puts up with modest gains, realizing that "the longest
journey starts with one step."
Hope accepts misunderstandings as the price for serving the
greater good of others.
Hope is a good loser because it has the divine assurance of
final victory.

"In this world you will have trouble, but be brave! I have defeated the world" (John 16:33 NCV).

There's almost an endless list of both negative and positive attitudes. However, I've simply lifted those few attitudes that seem to call for special caution or offer the best spirit for making retirement life's best chapter—including the minichapters within it.

Frank A. Clark wrote, "We've put more effort into helping folks reach old age than into helping them enjoy it." The right attitude may or may not lengthen your life, but it will put joy into your life. Age with attitude—the spirited attitudes for successful retirement.

REFLECTIONS AND PROJECTIONS

- Thinking back on your own life to this point, consider some either-or words to evaluate your attitude tendencies: Optimistic or pessimistic? Happy or sad? Bubbly or depressed? Doubtful or hopeful? Cynical or trusting?

- When have you liked yourself the best? The least? How well do you like yourself now?

- Assuming that you can choose attitudes that will alter your life, choose one attitude you most want to avoid in retirement. Now, choose one attitude you most want to cultivate in retirement.

- Based on your own self-image, what kind of attitude makeover do you see a need for? Outline your own makeover plan in writing, and put the plan where you'll see it and read it every single day.

RETIREMENT WORDS FROM THE WORD

Philippians 2:5; Ephesians 4:23; Galatians 4:18; Romans 12:3; Romans 12:2; Philippians 4:8

PRAYER THOUGHTS

Father, transform our minds so that our attitudes will reflect the attitudes of Jesus. Deliver us from the apathy of a whatever attitude, and help us to live spirited lives with can-do attitudes that come from knowing Your will and doing it in Your power. Help us retirees to have a sweet spirit instead of a sour one. May we be filled with enduring hope for the rest of our lives here until we're at home with You or Jesus returns as the blessed hope of us all. Amen.

CHAPTER FOURTEEN

OUTLIVING YOUR MONEY?

We all need money,
but there are degrees of desperation.

ANTHONY BURGESS

W hen retirement came suddenly, my income went down, but my quality of life went up. Although I was downsized from my job and the level of income I had expected to grow for another decade, I was upsized in many other ways. My career had been great, but it had been emotionally and physically taxing. In retirement, I found rest, new freedom, variety, flexibility, enjoyment, and the serendipity of being productive in ways that surprised me. My financial position was not as strong as I had expected it to be at retirement, but it was adequate then and continues to be adequate for the present.

Yet, at every turn it seems I run into the question, "Will you outlive your money?" It seems most books that deal with retirement focus heavily on financial matters or at least put them up front. Even though I know the importance of having enough money for retirement, I purposely chose to deal with finances toward the end of this book.

This book is primarily about retirement lifestyle and identifies with preacher Henry Ward Beecher, who wrote, "It is the heart that makes a man rich. He is rich according to what he is, not according to what he has." Even millionaire businessman Malcolm S. Forbes said, "The quality of life is in the mind, not in material."

Another part of my decision to delay dealing with finances goes back to something that happened once when I was in a small group discussing finances. A woman friend in her eighties had a twinkle in her eyes and a smile on her face as she said, "Money's not everything, but it's way ahead of whatever is in second place." This octogenarian's look, tone, and life actually said something different from her words to all of us in the room. She was actually saying that retirement and old age are not mainly about money. She was right, but she would also strongly agree that retirees need to be realistic about evaluating their financial needs and how to meet them.

CONTEXT FOR OUTLIVING YOUR MONEY

Many folks retire with a strong financial base; others are much less fortunate. These extremes are easy to document. According to the federal government's Administration on Aging, one of every six persons sixty-five or older was classified as *poor* or *near-poor* at the end of the twentieth century. Within that group, minorities and older women were more likely to be poor than older whites and older men. At the other end of the spectrum, 6 percent of those sixty-five or older reported incomes of fifty thousand dollars or more in 1998. And the economy's turns and downturns have negatively affected many who thought they retired well off enough to outlive their money.

The financial circumstances of retirees on both sides of age sixty-five vary dramatically. It's not my purpose to identify groups of retirees and levels of income; however, I cited statistics merely to confirm that in retirement, "We all need money, but there are degrees of desperation."

Without depreciating the circumstances of anyone, my purpose in this chapter is to point to some tips, testimonies, and attitudes toward financial health in retirement. I'm neither wealthy nor a financial advisor, but I believe I've got a fix on some approaches that will help answer the question about outliving your income. Further, I believe these approaches have something to say to those planning retirement, those just entering retirement, and those well into retirement.

TEN FINANCIAL GUIDELINES FOR RETIREMENT

My dad was fond of paraphrasing Will Rogers by saying, "Everybody's ignorant, just in different ways." He taught me to get expert help in areas of my ignorance, and I still practice what he taught me. So I asked the expert counsel of my own mentor, James W. Clark, for ten financial guidelines for retirement.

As a former corporate executive vice president, Jim was both a good steward in preparing financially for his own retirement and also in conscientiously working to help employees retire in good financial health. In retirement Jim worked part-time for a tax-consulting firm first and on the IRS's phone line later to help folks know how to complete their income tax reports. Although Jim is modest to a fault and doesn't claim to be a financial expert, he was glad to suggest these financial guidelines at my request and for your benefit.

Begin retirement planning early. Begin as early as practical, but, by all means, begin specific financial plans at least five years from retirement.

Analyze your current and projected financial position. (1) Consider current expenses—both what you spend and what you spend it for; and (2) consider what your preretirement income is and what your retirement income will likely be—assuming that life goes along pretty much as it is now. Specifically know these items: what your pension plan or other plans will pay you in retirement, what your Social Security benefits will likely be, any other income you can realistically expect in retirement, and any predictable cost reductions or increases in retirement.

Choose financial goals for yourself. But also enlist the help of trustworthy professionals or experienced people who can help you accomplish your goals. Those you look to for help might include a qualified financial advisor, a lawyer or tax attorney, and an accountant.

Make reasonable assumptions about inflation. Then build your financial plan accordingly. Inflation has been relatively mild for several years but goes up and down. It does compound, though; so if current trends continue, your fixed-income dollar might buy about 30 percent less in ten years than it does today. Although Social Security is now indexed to increase with inflation, your pension plan probably isn't indexed. That means what your pension was when you retired is probably what you're going to keep on getting.

Make a detailed list of all your assets. Then place a copy of this list with your will, or give a copy to those who will need to act in the event of your death or disability. The assets list needs to include everything financial: bank accounts, insurance policies, stocks, bonds, real estate, certificates of deposit, retirement accounts, and pension information.

Continue to invest in something. If at all possible in retirement, invest in something that will make you a little extra money. Try to put your money where it will earn at least 3 to 5 percent more than the Consumer Price Index (CPI) increases. Over the long term, stocks have done that and more; bonds have done so at times. And like investing in your children, financial growth investing is better over the long term than over the short haul. So be farsighted rather than shortsighted.

Plan to finance twenty or more years of retirement after age sixty-five. Because of increasing life spans, you might expect to live much longer than your parents or grandparents would have been expected to live when they were that age.

Plan for long-term health care. You may or may not need long-term care insurance, but without it, even well-off retirees can see their life savings disappear very rapidly. A counselor can help you evaluate this need based on your assets and other factors. There are many varied insurance plans available to meet potential needs for long-term health care.

Determine to live within your means now and in all of retirement. Discipline yourself to save something—regardless of how little or how much—for special things you want to do and also for investment. Develop a budget as a tool to manage and monitor your finances—not to follow slavishly but to look to if problems occur and corrections are necessary.

Use your credit wisely and to your benefit. Buy-now-pay-later is a good idea only if you buy what you need and what you can pay for on a timely basis *without accumulating interest or carrying charges.* Never pay only the minimum amount allowed on credit card debt! If possible, pay off the card every month, because interest wastes retirement dollars and is usually exorbitant.

REFLECTIONS ON THE TEN GUIDELINES

You and I may find ourselves editing the ten guidelines by altering, adding, or deleting to suit ourselves. Jim Clark would be the first to say that's okay, because they simply represent what he himself has gleaned over a lifetime from teachers, books, serving as corporate executive vice president, and other experiences.

On the other hand, who would be foolish enough to argue over the counsel to live within one's income? Calvin Coolidge said, "There is no dignity quite so impressive and no independence quite so important as living within your means."

As Jim and I discussed the ten guidelines, we talked about retirees who may lack expertise or inclination to do hands-on financial analysis and planning for themselves. Lots of folks just don't want to deal with dollars and cents even though common sense says they have to be dealt with. What then?

A stewardship requirement of life and possessions calls for retirees to do financial planning or to enlist someone to help them—and preferably a combination of the two. Although there are no guarantees about a long retirement life, God willing, a retiree might live another generation or so. And that potential calls for good financial preparation to go with all the other preparation we've talked about.

Just as I would be reluctant to put all of my financial eggs in one basket, I would be reluctant to put all my trust in one financial advisor. I would choose advisors from a reputable firm and from those with a proven history of both integrity and results.

I would be very cautious about Lone Ranger financial consultants. There is real wisdom in having a trusted and proven financial advisor. Left to ourselves, most of us may be too conservative or too radical in what we do with our retirement savings. A financial advisor can look at our goals, evaluate what we bring to the retirement table, ask questions, offer suggestions, and then explain possible consequences of the choices we make. Ultimately, though, it's your money and your decision.

Depending on your age and stage of retirement, it may be too late for you to do some of the early planning called for in the guidelines. Or you may not have had the luxury of retirement seminars and early planning because of sudden health factors, downsizing, business bankruptcy, or something else. Nevertheless, most of the guidelines are the kind you can begin to adopt right now. It's a good idea to move past regret over any past neglect of your financial planning or implementation.

My Own Financial Experience

As I've told you, I was retired considerably earlier than I had planned to retire—by five to ten years. But I didn't panic even though I had gotten a relatively late start in working toward retirement income. In fact, I was in my midthirties before I saved a dime toward retirement other than paying into Social Security. But even during hard times, I became aware of Catherine Crook de Camp's comment about money set aside for retirement savings: "Gone today, here tomorrow" (*The Money Tree*). And during my best income years, I made hay while the sun was shining as I saved and made investments.

Here are elements that were in my financial picture at retirement: (1) company pension/retirement plan; (2) a 401(k) savings plan matched with company funds; (3) a modest amount in an annuity fund; (4) an IRA—individual retirement account—invested in mutual funds; and (5) corporate payments equivalent to Social Security until I was eligible for Social Security.

Further, I felt confident I could continue to earn income without looking for other full-time work, and that confidence has proved to be well founded. Although I could no longer contribute to the company's 401(k) savings plan, a friend and my financial counselor introduced me to the government provision for a Simplified Employment Plan (SEP), which allowed me to add to my IRA account. The SEP allowed me a portion of my earnings as tax-deferred savings, and now there are other plans that allow for varied approaches to investing and taking best advantage of whether to delay taxes or pay them now. I didn't plan to retire from everything at once and haven't retired in that sense. So, although I'm retired, the term *semiretired* is more accurate or seems to fit better.

Since I retired with several income sources or benefits, it might sound as if I were rich. I wasn't—and I'm not—because the amounts were relatively modest; but I did follow sound financial counsel by diversifying savings with a view to retirement income needed. And in retirement, I've continued to try to save and invest some of our retirement resources.

While money is not everything, being freed from constant financial strain to meet most ongoing expenses has enabled me to be flexibly productive and happily varied in choices of how to spend retirement time. I find that I'm able to help others and minister in a way that I couldn't if I had to focus a disproportionate amount of retirement time on finances. Further, I've been able to say no to job offers or income possibilities that haven't suited me, and I've been able to say a glad yes to other opportunities that have come my way during retirement years.

There will likely come a time when I'm no longer able to earn money, or I just may not want to, but that time hasn't arrived yet. When and if such a time does arrive, I've made provisions for decisions that I myself may not be able to make at that stage of life. My mate, Phyllis, has interlocking provisions that match my own. Our Christian attorney helped us update our will—including a living will, durable power of attorney assignments, and the naming of executors of our estate. Copies of all those documents are on file with our attorney, with each of our children, and in our own possession.

We have tried to be good stewards of the possessions God has entrusted to us. And we have tried to prepare decently and in order for the time when that stewardship will pass to others.

Taking the Retirement Plunge

In all of life, most things we haven't experienced before bring a mixture of excitement and anxiety. Entering retirement can be that way. If one mate has been a homemaker and the other one out working and bringing home the bacon, entering retirement may be an especially anxious time for the homemaker.

Wives often reveal their anxiety by saying something like this: "We'll have to cut back, and we'll need to watch our money." Others may react to the mate's retirement suggestions by asking, "We can't afford that, can we?" For the one who has worked a lifetime to build a retirement nest egg to enjoy, those stated anxieties tend to put a burr under his or her saddle. Why? Probably because of a couple of things. The retiring mate probably doesn't like to hear what he or she feels are unfounded worries. Further, such statements may seem to reflect negatively on the retiring mate's financial planning. Or such comments may merely be received much like, "What's on your agenda today?" the question Phyllis asked me as my retirement dawned.

On the other hand, the mate retiring and returning to the home needs to be sensitive to the other mate's anxiety. If the income is going to be less than it has been in the past, it's a natural concern to wonder how the two of you will make it financially. It's good to have considered that question together before retirement; it's essential to consider the matter at the beginning of retirement. Mutual sharing about finances is helpful to both mates as they plan, monitor expenses, and move on, enjoying retirement. When both mates are retiring from income-producing work, financial understandings and agreements may be more complex and call for even more attention.

Typically, many expenses are deleted or reduced in retirement, and there's extra money to do some extra things. Unless there is lack of preparedness for retirement, catastrophic illness, or some other significant money drain, retirement lifestyle need not be a radical come-down from preretirement lifestyle. After plunging into retirement for a while and pausing to catch your breath, unfounded anxieties tend to go away or lessen. Of course, this varies from couple to couple and how well they have prepared financially for retirement.

THE STINGY-GENEROUS TENSION

Worry about money at the retirement plunge and after can lead to stinginess among those who have formerly been generous. The reason for backing away from tithing or charitable donations likely is rooted in a fear about financial security. Henry Ford said, "If money is your hope for independence you will never have it. The only real security that a man will have in this world is a reserve of knowledge, experience, and ability." Joe Louis said, "I don't like money, actually, but it quiets my nerves." And holding on to money instead of being charitable does seem to quiet some folks' nerves. But becoming small-souled, self-focused, and financially self-consumed is a high price to pay just to calm financial nerves.

The other tension has to do with how generous to be in retirement. My own parents kept right on tithing as they moved into retirement, and they were generous in other ways with their money. When Mother became a widow, she didn't quit tithing. In fact, Mother was generous to a fault on her small widow's pension and Social Security check despite heavy prescription bills for chronic medical conditions.

Besides all that, she was besieged with TV and junk mail pleas from ministries—worthy and otherwise—for as much of her money as they could get. She received special phone calls with tearful stories and urgent needs. And she gave to a number of those ministries. She never grew jaded or selfish.

Because of my own knowledge about cross-marketing and intensifying efforts to follow up on previous donors, I and my siblings realized Mother—like many other retirees—was being taken advantage of. And we set up some limits to safeguard Mother without unduly limiting her own independence. The government has helped with laws to protect privacy, but Mother's name and address still got around to a lot of organizations who are accountable for how they used her gifts. But for Mother herself, her gifts are registered in heaven because her motives were right.

On the other hand, Mother wasn't as naïve as we had earlier supposed. While she gave freely, she wasn't an easy mark for scam artists. For example, she got a call telling her she had won a twenty-five-thousand-dollar shopping spree. She told the caller she couldn't shop because she was legally blind and didn't need anything anyway. Good answer.

It's good not to become jaded or penny-pinching about appeals for gifts. On the other hand, it's wise to investigate causes and ministries before giving to them and avoid getting conned or taken into a scam. Retired couples would do well to have a buffer between them and those who would greedily take away their retirement savings. That buffer can be a family member or financial advisor that outsiders have to go through to get to the bulk of a retiree's or widow's savings. We can all use some financial counseling to conserve what we have for the use we saved it for, but the need for that help seems to increase with aging.

WHEN WIDOWHOOD COMES

Couples who cherish each other and their shared years of marriage don't even like to think about widowhood. Yet it is a fact of retirement and aging that relates to finances and needs advance consideration. As we entered the twenty-first century, there were roughly four times as many widows as widowers. On average, women outlive men by seven or eight years, and widows are more likely to live in poverty than widowers. So it's good to plan ahead.

Ideally, mates have equal knowledge and equal say in retirement finances. Then when one dies, the surviving mate will know all about their assets, liabilities, and all details related to financial concerns. But the ideal may be the exception rather than the rule on financial matters in marriages.

So in preparation for or as a result of being widowed, here are some things counselors suggest for a widowed person to do:

- Contact Social Security to be sure you're taking advantage of all the help available to you—both before and after widowhood. Ask for details on eligibility for Medicare, prescription programs, or other benefit programs that may come into being.
- If the spouse was a veteran, check for possible benefits for the widowed.
- Search all financial papers, files, and documents for overlooked assets or benefits.
- Contact the spouse's lawyer, banker, former employers, insurance companies, investment brokers, etc. Don't leave any financial stone unturned. If the widowed person isn't able to do these things personally, then the one who has power of attorney or another family member, advisor, or friend needs to offer this help.
- Don't make important financial decisions too quickly. For example, don't quickly sell your house, give away large sums of money, or retire from your previous lifestyle. Financial wisdom in widowhood is critically important. Time can be an ally in delaying major decisions beyond what has to be decided immediately. But timely decisions are important, too.

FOR THOSE WHO CAN'T RETIRE

For more reasons than I know of, many people feel they can't retire. They have deep business debts, lack of retirement savings and income, divorce repercussions, medical bills, or other circumstances that keep them at work beyond when they would like to retire. What can they do?

First, they may be able to retire and simply not know how to make that come to pass. The financial rite of passage from full-time employment to retirement may seem like a higher hurdle than it really is. Here's another example where good financial analysts or planners may be able to help find a way to retirement. Reduced income means less outgo in taxation and a number of other areas proportionately related to income. Debts might be consolidated with a reduction in both monthly payments and interest. A house might be refinanced at more favorable rates. And there are other recent options for improving the income and outgo balance of dollars.

Another consideration for those who think they can't retire may be that they have a misconception about retirement. Even for most people who can afford to retire, they find they need something to do besides indulge themselves. So they become semiretired or do something productive that continues to produce income. Those who feel they can't afford to retire may simply need to get a better concept of what retirement could be like. They may be able to cut back on hours or days of work or share a job to move into semiretirement.

One dictionary has *retool* after *retirement*. For those who approach a reasonable retirement age and are worn out in their jobs, they might consider retooling for some other enjoyable work that amounts to a type of retirement or semiretirement. A friend who worked for the same company for a full career also built up a lawn-service avocation. He decided to retire from his main job and just do the part-time job all the time. His seasonal occupation provides income, a variety of work, rest, and recreation, which I define as "productive retirement."

The beginning of this book suggests that retirees begin retirement with a sabbatical—a time of rest, a change of pace, a change of place for a while—and do something different. Even those who have to stay in the workplace might be able to plan more minisabbaticals or longer vacations and take time to smell the flowers before it is winter.

Retirement is not for everyone and is not possible for some. But the most enjoyable elements of retirement may also be available to those who continue to be part of the workforce.

Matching Money and Meaning

How much money does it take to enjoy a meaningful retirement? Although there are specialists who would suggest an answer to that question, the real answer is that it depends on what's meaningful to you and how well you match money to that meaning. What does life mean to you, and what does money mean to you?

Choice quotations I've read are thought provoking about the meaning of life and the meaning of money. Henry David Thoreau wrote, "Money is not required to buy one necessity of the soul." Bob Dylan said, "What's money? A man is a success if he gets up in the morning and gets to bed at night and in between does what he wants to do." Ralph Waldo Emerson wrote, "Money often costs too much." Patrick J. Buchanan observed, "To view poverty simply as an economic condition. . .is simplistic, misleading, and false; poverty is a state of mind, a matter of horizons." An anonymous person wrote, "Measure wealth not by the things you have, but by the things you have for which you would not take money." Ray Inman quipped, "The beauty of having a low income is that there is not enough money to buy what you don't really need." Bette Davis said, "To fulfill a dream, to be allowed to sweat over lonely labor, to be given a chance to create, is the meat and potatoes of life. The money is the gravy." Kate Seredy wrote, "I make money using my brains and lose money listening to my heart. But in the long run my books balance pretty well." Jonathan Swift concluded, "A wise man should have money in his head, but not in his heart."

Reflecting on Mother's life and rereading an e-mail I once got from my care-giving sister, Marylyn, I have a renewed sense about how much money it takes to enjoy a meaningful retirement. Here's what Marylyn wrote: "I called Mom and had a good visit. How can someone make little blue flowers in a flower bed and tomatoes growing on a vine sound like the Academy Awards? Isn't that wonderful?" Yes, it is wonderful.

You may have concluded that I have begged the question "Outliving your money?" If you were expecting a financial answer to the question, I would say your conclusion is right. However, I wrote with the thought that everyone ought to outlive their money. In other words, live above and beyond what money can buy and do.

When money has done all that it can do and must do for us in this life, it can't go beyond this life. As one preacher noted, "I've never seen a hearse with a U-Haul trailer behind it." My conviction is that you and I can go beyond this life and join the kind of treasure laid up for us in heaven. We can outlive our money both now and forever.

REFLECTIONS AND PROJECTIONS

- In all your life, recall when you have had the least money and the most money. What difference did the amount of money make to your happiness?
- Evaluate your past stewardship of money by considering these questions: Invested it? Buried it? Gained it? Lost it? Wasted it? Saved it? Gave it? Worshiped it? Used it? Thought too much of it? Thought too little of it? Had the right perspective and balance about it?
- How do you plan to use and invest your total assets for the next five years?
- If you or your spouse were to die today, would the surviving mate know the total financial picture and what actions to take? It would be a gift of love to make yes the answer to this question.

RETIREMENT WORDS FROM THE WORD

Luke 14:28; James 4:13–15; Matthew 25:21; Malachi 3:10; Matthew 6:20–21; Acts 20:35; Matthew 6:31–33

PRAYER THOUGHTS

Father, help us to be wise stewards of all we have and to trust You for all we need. Where there is poverty, help us to share from our resources. Help us not to bury our resources in fear or anxiety but to take considered risks and not waste opportunities to increase what You've entrusted to us. Help us to have the right perspective toward money and to use it well. And give us wisdom to outlive our money. Amen.

CHAPTER FIFTEEN

WRITING LIFE'S LAST CHAPTER

I am living in life's last chapter,
and it is best of all.

ELTON TRUEBLOOD

L ife is like a book, and it has to come to an end. At the end of this book, as at the beginning, I quote the late Elton Trueblood, who used that comparison when he told me, "Each chapter of life is good, and it is good to know in which chapter you are living. I'm living in life's last chapter, and it is best of all."

He held that conviction throughout his retirement. He was in his eighties when he shared that wisdom and testimony with me, and he died at ninety-four. The context for his writing was a rich lifetime of productivity that didn't end until he had finished writing life's last chapter—the one he called life's *best* chapter.

Elton's best and last chapter of life was a relatively long one that contained a number of minichapters. When that lengthy chapter of retirement climaxed the book of his earthly life, I wasn't there, but I believe he would have added an amen to his earlier conviction that the last chapter was best of all.

Trueblood wrote over thirty books, taught and mentored generations of students, traveled worldwide, performed a president's funeral, retired—or semiretired—and wrote his autobiography. As I've told you before, time and again he told me, "Johnnie, don't retire from everything at once. Rather, retire gradually from one thing at a time as you have to and want to." And that's what he did. His writing became newsletters instead of books. He gradually quit traveling to speak and teach but opened his home and heart and mind to those who came to him for mentoring. He did not leave life's last chapter unwritten.

Elton Trueblood was born in 1900, and he considered 1900 to still be part of the nineteenth century. His goal was to live at least until 2001 so he could say he had lived in three centuries. Although he missed his goal by several years, what he wrote etched the book of his life into eternity. And now he lives beyond time.

It is his kind of model that inspires me and also makes me want to encourage others to write all of life's last chapter with excellence—an excellence that deserves the title "Life's Best Chapter." And my wanting the last to be the best includes this book's final part, which I've titled "Writing Life's Last Chapter."

When a friend asked me about my book on retirement, I told him I had written it about retirement being life's best chapter. Upon hearing that, he looked into my eyes and asked, "And have you found it to be the best?" I was glad to say yes—so far. And I told him why. What I told him is what this chapter is about.

LIFE'S BEST CHAPTER?

How can the last chapter of life be the best one since it ends in death? Realistically, we have to admit that our bodies are wearing out as we groan with arthritis or some other *itis*. Most of us struggle in one way or another as we try to see, hear, chew, move around, remember, and stay in charge of our lives. Life's early physical pleasures eventually diminish, and we're challenged in new ways almost every day. So how can retirement really be life's best chapter? What about writing the last part of the last chapter?

I can't honestly say that retirement is the best chapter of life for everyone. That would be inaccurate. In fact, the last chapter may be the worst chapter for many. So experiencing retirement as the best chapter—the dessert chapter—of life is not automatic and calls for a lot of effort.

Writing the retirement chapter of life and making it the best of all chapters calls for wisdom, commitment, perspective, energy, endurance, and undying faith in the Author and Finisher of our faith. With those givens, retirement truly can be life's best chapter all the way to the end. And so far that's my testimony from personal experiences and observation of Elton, Mother, and others.

WAYS THE LAST CHAPTER IS BEST

Someone wrote, "The pleasures of old age are not less than those of youth, but they are different." I tend to agree with that statement. To me, in some ways, the difference in younger years and older years is like stew. A new batch of stew tastes good, but later warm-ups of that same stew move from good to delicious as more seasoning takes place. The last chapter of life is well seasoned, but it also has new ingredients that make it different. With these thoughts in mind, here are some ways that the last chapter of life seems best to me.

The last chapter builds on other chapters and becomes climactic. Just as we dread coming to the end of a great book we're reading, we're not ready to finish the book of our lives on earth. But part of reading a book is coming to the end and finishing it. So the last chapter of life is a natural part of the book that provides completion. "Writing Life's Last Chapter" is about everything I've said to you so far and also about bringing the earthly book of life to a climactic end. We don't want the book to end. But it has to. And how the book ends is important—contrary to those who say it doesn't matter how you die but rather how you live. The whole book matters all the way to the end.

The last chapter is shalom! As I understand it, this Hebrew greeting is a wish for peace, but it is more than a wish for the absence of conflict. It is also a wish for God's highest blessings. The last chapter of life can reach a new level of *shalom*—peace and blessings—after the storms. Although there are storms of life in retirement, life no longer tends to be like living in Tornado Alley. We're not caught up in many of the traumas that buffet life during the earlier years.

Someone once said that he didn't mind the rat race but would like to have more of the cheese. Regardless of how much or little cheese we have, the rat race is mostly over for most retirees. The hurry of life is over. My dad never did like to have to hurry. And in retirement, when anyone tried to rush him, he would reply, "If I had known I was going to have to hurry, I would have started sooner." That was his way of saying that he wasn't going to hurry. And he didn't have to.

Most of the retirees I know enjoy the relative peace of the last chapter. They tend to take the roads less traveled and often depart from the interstates and those who always seem to be in a tailgating rush. In retirement, most of us find it easier to let God be our pacesetter and our pacemaker.

The last chapter is filled with optional time. Actually, all of life is optional time since no one can enslave our conscience, and we can choose all of life in that sense. But the earlier chapters of life tend to be tied to a sense of *have-to* rather than *want-to* in a lot of what we do. In retirement, there is a special sense of freedom in choosing what to do with time.

Opportunities pop up everywhere, and they're not just obstacles or problems under the name of issues. Retirees who want to can pursue their curiosities, try something new and different, travel near or far, gain new skills, become a Good Samaritan instead of a passerby priest or Levite, and say yes or no to requests for their time.

About the time Mother became an octogenarian, she began to say with a lilt in her voice, "We can just do what we want to." That hadn't been true for most of her life. As the eldest of eight children in a farm family, she was almost a co-mother in raising her siblings. And with brief respite at marriage, she began to raise her own children until life's chapter finally offered more free time. Even then, what she chose to do with her heart was mostly to help others in any way she could.

The last chapter is harvest time for satisfaction. Wise retirees let regrets sift through the sieve of life, and they prefer to focus on recalling the satisfactions of life's experiences. Despite the problems that occur in each succeeding generation of a family, there is a joy when we retirees see part of our best genes at work in our children, grandchildren, and great-grandchildren. With this satisfaction, we realize that in a sense the last chapter will not be the end of our lives on earth even after we're gone.

This satisfaction benefit of retirement is reserved for those whose thanksgiving for blessings is greater than their griefs over losses in life or the scars of life.

The last chapter is time to celebrate the present. The past and future are important seasons of life, but we often let them steal the present moment. As I have listened to people the world over, I have heard them worship a golden past or a utopian future—each of which likely never is a part of reality.

In the changing seasons of each year, I've noticed that comments I make about enjoying the present season often draw a contrary response from others. For example, if I comment on the beauty of spring, the warmth of summer, the fresh air of fall, or the beauty of a snowfall, someone usually differs with me. They express a preference for a past season or one yet to come over the present season. To me, it's really sad for a person not to enjoy the present seasons of life.

Retirement is both the autumn and sunset of life. It is a time to celebrate without letting anyone steal the present. Although winter and darkness come next, it is a waste to let the autumn go unappreciated or the thought of darkness ruin the sunset. Furthermore, after each winter there is springtime, and after each night, there is a sunrise. The Christian retiree knows that the same will be true for his life after this life. But, for now, it's time to celebrate the present.

These are just a few of the many ways that the last chapter can be the best of all chapters. But there are some more valuable tips on how to go about writing life's last chapter. So let's take a look at them.

SAYING YES TO ALL OF LIFE

Psychologist Paul Tournier was convinced that those who write the earlier chapters of life positively and successfully are most likely to do a great job writing life's last chapter. His reference point for success wasn't a person's title, money, fame, name, health, or other circumstance. Rather, his reference point was whether a person chooses to live each stage of life fully and say yes to all of it.

Tournier saw the successful writing of the last chapter of life as the final *yes* in life. He put it this way in his book *Learn to Grow Old*: "A single *yes* goes through the whole of life. It is successively *yes* to childhood, to youth, to adult life, to old age, and finally *Yes!* to death. It is easier to turn over a page of life when we have filled it right up." The Bible talks of the patriarchs who died in peace because they had lived their full span of years (Genesis 25:8). Tournier wrote both out of experience and conviction when he stated, "My old age has meaning. I can live through it with my gaze still fixed before me, and not behind me, because I am on my way to a destination beyond death" (*Learn to Grow Old*).

One bad page or one bad chapter doesn't necessarily make a bad book. Ideally, a book is consistently good from beginning to end. But as we write the book of our lives, none of us is perfect, so there are bad pages and bad chapters in it. Yet there are people who have learned to fully affirm the facts of each chapter of life with a *yes* and to move on to the next chapter. Those are the ones inclined to say *yes* to life's last chapter—including death—and to write it well.

For those who haven't said *yes* to each stage of life, there is still hope as they come to life's last chapter. This hope requires a conversion, a transformation, an about-face that moves from the negative to the positive. The kind of change I'm talking about is not possible for the individual to make alone. Rather, it is the experience of coming to know God in Christ as personal Lord and Savior (see John 3:16–18; Romans 10:9–13; Ephesians 2:8–10).

When a person quits saying *no* to God and surrenders with a trusting *yes* to God's gift of grace, it is then that he is born again and is transformed (John 3:1–10; Romans 12:1–2). It is best to learn to say this *yes* early in life; but if that experience hasn't occurred by retirement, it is essential for the birth of hope in life's last chapter and beyond. Now is the time to say *yes* to God and to the rest of life. Then the end of life's book will not be the end of life; rather, the first book will be far surpassed by its sequel in eternal life—which begins with *yes* and never ends.

Living beyond Your Age

What is your RealAge? A friend of mine introduced me to an Internet site that had a quick test to estimate biological *RealAge* against chronological age. I answered the questions on the test as honestly as I could at my present chronological age. Then I almost immediately got the evaluation that my biological RealAge was 3.2 years younger than my chronological age. Most of us retirees like to hear that we're younger than we are—whether it's an estimation based on scientific data or whether someone just tells us that we look younger than we are. But my RealAge barely brought a smile to my face, because I know about the brevity of life, about mortality, and that life is much more than the number of calendar years we live.

Consider your mortality. As in all of life, people in retirement die at different ages. Unless someone takes his own life, it is anyone's guess when a person will inspire (breathe in) for the last time and expire (breathe out in death) for the last time. In an average lifetime of seventy-eight years, there are 683,280 hours or 2.4 billion seconds. At 8,760 hours per year, it doesn't take long to estimate how much time you might have left.

Interestingly, it seems most folks don't look at how long they've lived as much as they consider how much life they have left. And while most people would like to live a long life, some of them don't know what to do with themselves on a rainy afternoon.

Learn about quality of life. Although the length of life is uncertain, facing death is certain. None of us can choose how long we will live, but we can choose how we write today's page and this last chapter we're living in. The quantity of life—figured biologically or by the calendar—is not nearly as important as the quality of life and the contribution of a life.

Writing life's last chapter well—regardless of how long or short the chapter is—depends on the daily stands we take, the convictions we hold, and the choices we make. The point is this: Don't let the condition of your body or the number of years you live determine your quality of life.

Take Charge of Life's Last Chapter

Choose life. Some retirees choose to withdraw from active life and live with shriveled-up spirits long before physical death occurs. They choose a kind of living death before the funeral instead of choosing life in the face of death. I agree with what Jack London wrote: "The proper function of man is to live, not to exist. I shall not waste my days trying to prolong them. . . . I shall use my time" (*The Book of Positive Quotations*).

The Bible itself says, "I have set before you life and death. . . therefore choose life" (Deuteronomy 30:19 KJV). In retirement we can choose to write the last chapter with life rather than death—as climax rather than anticlimax. The choice is ours.

Seize life's opportunities. The condition of a person's inner spirit is above and beyond biology and chronology in determining the value of a person's life. To say it another way, great-souled people stay young despite aging bodies, and they live decisive, positive lives. In the Greek language, there are two words for time: *chronos* and *kairos*. *Chronos* is any old time—just a chronicle or chronology of life. But *kairos* means opportune time. The person whose inner spirit stays young and alive keeps on making timely decisions that result in life's super moments. And as long as a person lives and chooses, it's never too late to have one of life's super moments that redeem the time (Ephesians 5:15–16).

Don't let dying stop your living. Sociology professor Morrie Schwarz had seemingly said *yes* to all the chapters in life when he was diagnosed with Lou Gehrig's disease (amyotrophic lateral sclerosis—ALS). The diagnosis was a death sentence because this disease would slowly and agonizingly waste Morrie's body from legs to lungs until it would kill him. He would begin to lose the use of his body but not his mind.

Morrie had been the professor, mentor, and friend of Mitch Albom, who became an award-winning writer. Twenty years after Mitch's college experience and awhile after Morrie had contracted ALS, Mitch reconnected with Morrie for one final, informal course on living and dying. The book *Tuesdays with Morrie* grew out of that course.

In effect, Morrie was writing life's last chapter, and he knew the chapter would be a short one. Besides all the other feelings and emotions Morrie had, he decided early on whether to withdraw and die or to live life as fully as possible in the time he had left. He chose life. He chose to live as long as possible with dignity, courage, humor, composure, and love. He refused to be ashamed of dying, and he refused to equate dying with uselessness. He did not see dying as a reason to quit living.

With a lack of self-pity and a refusal to surrender to depression, Morrie began what might be considered his best chapter of life as a professor. He said that everyone knows he or she going to die but that no one believes it. He shared what he himself had experienced: that when you have come face-to-face with death and learned not to fear it, then you're freed to live.

Morrie became a catalyst to teach and challenge people to separate the wheat from the chaff in life and to learn how to get meaning into their lives. He taught that the last chapter is not too late to get involved in life. The way Morrie wrote that last chapter of life challenges all of us as we write our own last chapter. Life's last chapter can be magnificent.

Decide how busy you will be. Perhaps there ought to be an eleventh commandment for retirees, namely this: "Thou shalt not say you're so busy you don't know when you had time to work." I answer questions about how busy I am by saying I'm not any busier than I want to be.

Retirees have more optional time than ever, but the quantity of leisure time often seems to make it harder than ever to organize and manage time productively. The fact that time is limited is no reason to crowd it with activities that seemingly have no priority. We live life's last chapter best when we choose to pace ourselves.

Good time management avoids a crushing schedule that

produces anxiety or emotional claustrophobia. Good steward-ship of time is the deliberate choice to live life decently and in order by giving priority to what is most meaningful in life. It's true that some chapters of life are busier and more hectic than others, but it is equally true that personal choice affects our own attitude about how busy we are. And this fact especially applies to retirement.

Again and again, my mind has gone back to the brevity of Jesus' life and His awareness of how brief His time on earth would be. At about age thirty, He fully knew He was living life's last earthly chapter. Yet He who was so busy never seemed to rush and never counted Himself too busy to help others. He who was dying said, "I am the way, the truth, and the life" (John 14:6 KJV). In obedience to His Father, He said *yes* to every chapter of life and chose to write the last chapter with life both for Himself and for all of us. Jesus lived life productively, positively, decisively, and timely.

GET YOUR AFFAIRS IN ORDER

When I was a Boy Scout, I learned a valuable lesson for all of life: "Be prepared!" Although the motto is a good one for all of life, it's critically important for life's last chapter.

Check your spiritual life. I've shared in an earlier chapter the experience I once had on a jetliner. The pilot came on the inter-com and told us we would need to prepare for a crash landing because of a possible malfunction in the landing gear. As we circled the airport to use up fuel, I began to check my spiritual life. I was ready to live or die because I had already accepted Christ as Lord and Savior. Fortunately, the landing gear held and we landed safely; but my peace and ultimate safety hadn't depended on landing gear. It had depended on my relationship to God in Christ. This preparation has priority over all other affairs that need to be in order.

When Henry David Thoreau was dying, a priest asked him if he had made his peace with God. Thoreau answered, "I was not aware that we had quarreled." Everyone has quarreled with God and His will and needs to make peace with Him (see Isaiah 53:6; Romans 3:23, 6:23, 10:9–10).

Check your human relationships. Is everything all right between you and the rest of your family? Or do you need to ask for or give forgiveness? Are your friendships in good repair? Is there anything you want to say to someone or do for them before life's last chapter closes? Now is the time to speak and act. Then there won't be any regrets. When Dad died, I spoke at his funeral. And I was glad to be able to say our family didn't have any regrets: We had pretty well said or done all that we needed to while Dad was still with us. Dad left heritage, legacy, quotations, and memories. And though he has gone to be with the Lord, in a sense he's still with us because of what he left us. And the same thing is true of Mother, who died more recently.

Check your financial matters. Is your will up to date? Are your bills paid or provided for in your estate? Does your spouse know what the widowed survivor's financial condition will be? Have you chosen an executor for your estate, and are you satisfied with that choice? If you were left behind to settle your own estate, are things the way you would like for them to be? You may want to update some things, share some financial information with family members or others, collect financial records and put them together in one place. And if all that seems like too much trouble, you might just want to enlist someone to do the detail work to your satisfaction.

Make your wishes known. Besides having a formal will, there's a certain satisfaction in passing on possessions to the ones you would like to have them. There may be diaries or journals that need to be available to all family members and preserved as a part of family heritage and history. I've kept a diary most of my life, and one of my reasons for that discipline has been to share the writing of my life with my descendants as they write the books of their lives.

In living life's last chapter, there ought not be anything morbid or foreboding about sharing what you would like to happen after you die. Morris Schwarz decided to have a living funeral for himself. He invited those he wanted to be there, and he decided what would take place. So though he was still alive, he conducted his own funeral.

But most of us leave our funeral to others. They would probably appreciate knowing our wishes and would likely find comfort and joy in trying to carry out those wishes—assuming the wishes are reasonable ones. Some of our wishes might include who would perform the funeral, favorite songs and scriptures, and place of burial. In our society, cremation has become a more popular choice in recent years. Some family members might be bothered with this personal choice. So it's a good idea to be especially sensitive in sharing with other family members if this should be your choice.

There may be other affairs you need to get in order or want to get in order. In life's last chapter, there is a special joy in being prepared.

EXCHANGE YOUR TENT FOR A MANSION

We all have an earthly body that grows older and eventually wears out. The apostle Paul wrote about it in 2 Corinthians 4:16–5:10. Paul made tents with his own hands. He compared the body to a tent, and in those days, tents were usually made of skin. For Christians, he was confident that the earthly tent would be exchanged for a house not made with hands and would be fit for all eternity.

Jesus spoke of that house as a mansion (John 14:2 KJV). Contemporary Bible scholars often translate this verse with terms such as *dwelling places* or *rooms* instead of *mansions*. But I like the question one preacher asked about the matter: "Can you imagine a house in heaven being less than a mansion?" And I myself prefer to think of it as exchanging a tent for a mansion.

Once I was teaching my married couples' Bible class from the passage Paul wrote about the tent wearing out. Now, I knew how class member Judy Cooper had felt about the leaky-tent-camping-out honeymoon experience husband Jerry had taken her on. So I had prompted Judy to tell the class about it to illustrate the point I wanted to drive home. Judy shared in detail all the misery and discomfort of living in a leaking tent in the wilds of Canada. Then I made my point: "You see, a tent gets old, wears out, and is not as good as a house." Unprompted, Judy added, "And the tent never was as good as a house."

She taught me, her teacher, a great lesson: *No matter how great or good an earthly body is at any stage of life on earth, it is never as good as the resurrection body God has in store for us.*

Consider what your body was like during the stages of your earthly life. What stage of your earthly body would you like for your resurrection body to reflect? Certainly not as it is in the last chapter. But also, not as it was in any earlier chapter of life.

Without losing our personality and without losing what lets others recognize us, God plans to replace our destroyed tent with a mansion fit for all eternity. That mansion will be better than the earthly tent ever was at any stage of our existence. And it's hard to imagine God would do any less for the mind.

So we don't need to worry about what our body loses and the destruction that comes. We don't need to worry about bodies destroyed in accidents, burned up in fires, or vaporized in acts of terrorism. God will replace our earthly tents with His heavenly mansions.

Life is a book, and retirement can be its best chapter. The last chapter may be short or long, but it will likely be made up of a number of minichapters. No matter what we decide to do with retirement, we are still responsible to God for being good stewards of His calling. The Bible challenges us to "walk worthy of the calling wherein you are called" (Ephesians 4:1, my translation). Writing the last chapter of life continues to be a stewardship that we are entrusted with by the "author and the finisher of our faith" (Hebrews 12:2 KJV).

Although retirement is a time for rest, recreation, and leisure, it is also a time for recreation, productivity, and continuity in letting our lives be living letters written with the Spirit of the living God (2 Corinthians 3:2–3). In the last analysis, God will judge for each of us whether retirement was life's best chapter. If we choose God as our coauthor and write it according to His will, there's a good chance retirement will be life's best chapter.

As I finish writing this book and you finish reading it, I pray that the effort we've both made will make life's last chapter grander and will also get us ready for the sequel—to be written in heaven.

REFLECTIONS AND PROJECTIONS

- Identify something in the book that has already made a difference in your retirement life.
- Think through the last chapter of this book and reflect on how you're writing life's last chapter in the book of your life.

I didn't write this book just to write a book; I wrote it to make a difference in the lives of those who read it. For that reason, join with me in some assumptions and suppositions that could make a difference in your life.

- Assume that life's last chapter for you will contain at least five minichapters of one year each. Identify one priority, project, or activity you would like to write with your life in each of those five years.
- Assume that life's last chapter for you is one year from now. Make a checklist from this chapter and from your own mind and heart of what you want to get in order to complete the book of your life. Commit to do at least one of those items on your checklist this week.
- If you were asked to rewrite this book on retirement, what would you add to the book to make retirement life's best chapter? List at least one or two items. Then make sure your life matches what you have added—or plan steps to make the items part of your last chapter.
- Suppose an editor asked you to write a book on retirement that majored on hope, joy, productivity, and positive living. And suppose the book had to come from your own retirement experiences. Could you do it? Or what would have to change for you to be able to write such a book?
- Now, from one author to another author, here's my final

suggestion: Get a journal and start a literal writing of your life's last chapter. And determine to make it life's best chapter. Happy writing.

RETIREMENT WORDS FROM THE WORD

1 Peter 3:15; Genesis 25:8; Deuteronomy 30:19–20; Ephesians 5:15; 2 Corinthians 3:2–3; 2 Corinthians 5:1; 2 Peter 1:13–15; 1 Corinthians 15:22, 26; 2 Timothy 4:6–8

PRAYER THOUGHTS

Father, help us to enjoy the blessings of retirement and be aware of our stewardship responsibility to live it productively all the way to the end of this earthly life. May we have wisdom not to retire from everything at once, motivation to continue choosing life, and courage to face dying without giving up living. May we trust You to help us complete our book of life and fulfill Your promise to exchange ours tents for mansions. Amen.

The Student Bible Dictionary
Communication Skills: Clearly Making a Difference
Syzygy: How to Live a Powerfully-Aligned Life
What It Means to Be Born Again (Spanish edition)

Also from Barbour Publishing

Living Life to the Max

by Vernon Armitage and Mark Littleton
Through insightful scriptures, relevant examples, and
practical applications, *Living Life to the Max* puts at
readers' fingertips God's how-to principles for living
the life He created to the fullest.
ISBN 1-59310-066-3
224 pages

Living a Life of Hope

by Nathan Busenitz
Living a Life of Hope helps readers shift their gaze from the
"here and now" to the wonders of "forever" for a life of
greater purpose, power, and joy.
ISBN 1-58660-983-1
256 pages

Outdoors with God

by Lance Moore
Quiet-time inspiration finds truth in God's Word—
and nature.
ISBN 1-58660-919-X
224 pages

Men Are Clams, Women Are Crowbars

by David Clarke, PhD
Dr. David Clarke details the divergent ways men and
women approach emotional issues, then offers solutions
for couples who want to bridge the gender gap.
ISBN 1-58660-726-X
256 pages